Victorian and Edwardian

Country-House Life

from old photographs

Victorian and Edwardian

Country-House Life

from old photographs

Anthony J. Lambert

B.T. Batsford Ltd
London

For Rosemary and Ian with gratitude

First published 1981
Reprinted 1984
© Anthony J. Lambert 1981

ISBN 0 7134 1737 4

Filmset in Monophoto Apollo by
Servis Filmsetting Ltd, Manchester

Printed and bound in Great Britain by
Anchor Brendon Ltd, Tiptree, Essex
for the publishers B. T. Batsford Ltd
4 Fitzhardinge Street, London W1H 0AH

Frontispiece: Breakfast at Sunningdale Park, Berkshire,
*c.*1889, taken by Alexandra, Princess of Wales who was
a keen amateur photographer. From left to right are
Maria, Marchioness of Ailesbury, Princess Victoria of
Wales and the Hon. Julie Stonor, daughter of Lord
Camoys. Georgina Sophia Maria was the wife of the 5th
Marquess of Ailesbury, who was M.P. for Wiltshire at
the time of this photograph, and daughter of G.H.
Pickney of Tawstock Court, Devon. It was not
uncommon for the aristocracy to enjoy the comfort of a
private waiting room at their local station, but the
Marquess of Ailesbury had the rare privilege of a private
station at Great Bedwyn on the Great Western Railway.
He was entitled to request stops at his convenience.
Breakfast was then a substantial meal with cooked dishes
resembling today's mixed grill.

Reproduced by gracious permission of
Her Majesty the Queen

Right: Not a country house, but a meeting in 1894 of
inestimable significance for the future of many houses.
Alfriston Clergy House was a fourteenth-century
dwelling for a small community of parish priests, and by
the nineteenth century it had been converted into
labourers' cottages. It was in a dilapidated state by the
time this small group of concerned people gathered
together to see what could be done to save it. The
National Trust was not an official body when this
photograph was taken but two years later, Alfriston
Clergy House became the Trust's first historic building,
bought for the princely sum of £10. Money to restore
the building was the objective of the Trust's first appeal;
mercifully for the nation's heritage it was a success.

The National Trust

Contents

Acknowledgments   vi

Foreword   vi

Introduction   vii

Photographs and commentaries   xi

Acknowledgments

In the course of researching this book, I have received much kindness and generous hospitality from many people and I am glad to have this opportunity of thanking them: the Marchioness of Aberdeen, Mr A.J. Adam, Mr P.N. Allen, the Marquess of Anglesey, the Duke of Atholl, Mr J. Baldwin, Lord Barnard, Miss Francesca Barran, Mr J.M. Blake, Miss Camilla Bowyer, the Duke of Buccleuch, Mr P.R. Burkett, Mr Hugh Cavendish, the Earl of Cawdor, Mr G. Clarke, Sir John Clerk, Mr S.F.B. Cordrington, Mr W.J. Connor, Mr S. Croad, Miss F. Dimond, Miss M.E.G. Dorehill, Mr I. Dougall, the Earl of Elgin, Mr N.A. Foster, Mr J.D. Galbraith, Mr R.M. Gard, Mr P. Grant, Mr F. Hackett, Lt Commander J. Hamilton, Miss J. Hardy, the Earl of Harrowby, Mr A.D. Hill, Mrs B. Holden, Mr F.A. Hudson, Mr F.C. Jolly, the Earl of Kintore, Mr R. Lassam, Sir Michael Leighton, Mrs M.B. Longley, the Hon. David Lytton Cobbold, Mr W.R. MacDonald, Mr J.A. Maddox, Mrs P. Maxwell-Scott, Sir Stephen Middleton, Mr C. Milne, Mr M.S. Moss, Miss J. Mundy, Mrs S. Pettit, the Earl of Pembroke, Mr J.R. Reynolds, Lord Saye & Sele, Mr F. Sayer, Mr W. Serjeant, Lord Skelmersdale, Miss E. Steele, Dr M. O'Sullivan, Mr M.L. Tebbutt, Col A. R. Waller, Dr S.B. Ward, Mr J.M. Waterson, Mr L. White, Mrs F.M. Williams, and Mrs M. Willis. To Her Majesty the Queen and the various public bodies and institutions who have kindly granted permission to use photographs in their collections, I extend my thanks. I would also like to thank the staff of the many public libraries who kindly helped in finding often obscure information in old newspapers. My thanks to Michael Dunn and Sue Cleave for their helpful proof reading. Finally, I am grateful to Tish Cargill for much help and to the publishers for their patience and help.

Foreword

It has been the intention in compiling and writing this book, to give a broad portrayal of country-house life, both through the pictures themselves and through brief biographies of some of the people in or connected with them. Old photographs can be meaningless or lacking in interest without some background information about the person, the occasion or the building. Wherever possible, this has been given.

Introduction

At the beginning of Victoria's reign, the country house was the symbol and expression of power with which people were most familiar. The vast majority of the population lived and worked in the countryside and, with limited scope or need for travel, had no experience of a further dimension to eclipse the importance of their local landowner and his estate. Moreover he was the focal point of the community to an extent which is now difficult to visualise, often dispensing law, charity, education, command of the militia or yeomanry and, on occasions, hospitality. Land and power were virtually synonymous for it was only during the nineteenth century that commercial success provided a common avenue to political eminence. On the rare occasions that peers were created from landless families, it was considered only proper that sufficient funds should accompany the honour to purchase an estate. Wellington was able to purchase Stratfield Saye with the money given him with his peerage, and as late as 1919, Haig was given £100,000 with his earldom. The political influence associated with land was assaulted but far from destroyed by the 1832 Reform Bill, although by the end of the Edwardian era there was but a vestige of the power exercised over parliamentary elections by landowners in 1837.

Similarly, the functions and traditional responsibilities of the country gentleman in his community were eroded and institutionalised. As G.E. Mingay has written, 'the intimate paternalism of the old order gave way to the impersonal, remote control of the state.' The amateur, unpaid administrators were slowly compelled to relinquish their positions, although the first elections to county councils in 1888 saw many a landowner returned. Until the creation of county councils, the justices of the peace, who were usually drawn from the gentry and clergy, supervised jails, arranged road and bridge repairs, and dealt with minor offences in the special 'Justice Room' with which some country houses were equipped. Where landowners were absent from their estates, the regimen for tenants and agricultural workers could undoubtedly be severe if immediate income was the prime concern of the agent. But landowners were usually more in touch with the reality of agrarian economics and too concerned with the long-term prosperity of their estates to prejudice the future for present gain. Rents were often waived in times of hardship, or subsidised from other income, as in the case of the Marquess of Bute who used revenue from Cardiff docks and coal mines to keep down the rents of his Glamorgan tenants. Equally, absentee or uninterested landowners were rare in England, unlike their counterparts in France where Paris and high society dominated their outlook. As the American Ambassador to Britain wrote in 1819, 'the permanent interests and affections of the most opulent classes here centre almost universally in the country. They have *houses* in London . . . but their *homes* are in the country.' The Duke of Devonshire sold his historic house in Piccadilly for £1 million before parting with an acre of Derbyshire countryside. And of course there were model landlords – Lord Wantage provided his villagers at Ardington and Lockinge with schools, well-built roomy cottages, a co-operative retail store, a savings bank and friendly society, and made the tenant of *The Bull* offer soup, tea and coffee besides alcohol. He even introduced a profit-sharing scheme for his labourers and continued to afford improvements after the agricultural depression affected the industry.

On occasions, the villagers on and around an estate would be allowed to pass the heavy iron gates and lodge to share in the celebration of an important event for the family – a twenty-first birthday of the heir or a wedding. But for the *hoi polloi* to penetrate the façade of high society was another matter; the cardinal sin for an aristocrat was conduct which would lead to a public exposure of anything that could be the subject of ridicule or contempt. The veneer must never be cracked. Since it was expected of one to set an example, the guiding principle was: 'Thou shalt not be found out.' The extent to which the moral climate deteriorated under the unacknowledged influence of Edward when Prince of Wales is easy to exaggerate. The gentry were largely un-affected and the aristocracy divided by cliques and sets. Nonetheless, if it was reasonable to look to the aristocracy as the inspiration for a broad high-mindedness and a source of patronage for the arts, there is little doubt that there was a marked decline in the expression of these ideals during the late Victorian and Edwardian eras. In his *Experiment in Autobiography* H.G. Wells wrote:

> It is one of my firmest convictions that modern civilisation was begotten and nursed in the households of the prosperous, relatively indepen-dent people, the minor nobility, the gentry, and the larger bourgeoisie. . . . Within these households, behind their screen of deer park and park wall and sheltered service, men could talk, think and write at their leisure. They were free from inspection and immediate imperatives. . . . They could be inter-ested in public affairs without being consumed by them. The management of their estates kept them in touch with reality without making exhaustive demands on their time. Many, no doubt, de-generated into a life of easy dignity or gentlemanly vice, but quite a sufficient number remained curious and interested to make, foster and protect the accumulating science and literature of the seventeenth and eighteenth centuries. Their large rooms, their libraries, their collections of pictures and 'curios' retained into the nineteenth century

an atmosphere of unhurried liberal enquiry, of serene and determined insubordination and per-sonal dignity, of established aesthetic and intel-lectual standards. Out of such houses came the Royal Society, the *Century of Inventions*, the first museums and laboratories and picture galleries, gentle manners, good writing, and nearly all that is worth while in our civilisation today.

The outlook at the beginning of the nineteenth century was promising: intellectuals proliferated on the public scene, and lively published debates between some of the characters depicted by Hazlitt in *The Spirit of the Age* were more than cloistered academic controversies; the excite-ment created by the prospect of rapid scientific discovery and industrial progress added a new dimension for the curious spirit. The relationship between the aristocracy and intellectuals, writers and artists was one of ease and cordiality, and one which reflected the interests and preoccupations of the aristocracy over previous centuries: Lucy, Countess of Bedford, was patroness of Donne and other poets; Pope consorted with the Earl of Burlington and Lord Bathurst; Dryden and Ad-dison were employed by Lord Halifax, founder of the Bank of England; and Canaletto was helped on his arrival in England by the 4th Duke of Richmond. The reasons for the growing worldli-ness and philistinism amongst a prominent sec-tion of the aristocracy cannot be examined here; we can only note that contemporaries were dismayed by the tendencies they saw around them. Lord Ernest Hamilton labelled the mid-Victorian era as an 'age of amiable humbug', and the value ascribed to intellectual and aesthetic qualities diminished. Concern with taste and the fruits of an inquiring mind gave way to an anachronistic interest in chivalry and noble conduct, fostered at best by Walter Scott and at worst by the contemporary equivalent of inferior paperbacks. For a late Victorian example of the commitment and interest given by Beckford to the creation of Fonthill, one has to look to a *nouveau riche* like William Armstrong rather than an aristocrat. As Victoria's reign progressed, the moral earnestness and seriousness gave way to a more flippant and liberal, if hypocritical, ambiance, engendered by 'the society of fashionable and fast people', as Her Majesty phrased it. In Vita Sackville-West's *The Edwardians*, the explorer Anquetil, an outsider who has been invited to Chevron for a weekend, is amazed by the puerile banter: 'Here are a score or more of people . . . who by virtue of their position are accustomed to the intimate society of princes, financiers, wits, beauties, and other makers of history, yet are apparently content with desultory chatter and make believe occupation throughout the long hours of an idle day.' For his hostess, 'as to most of her acquaintance, the life of pleasure was all in all, neither books, art, nor music meant anything to her except in so far as their topicality formed part of the social equipment.'

There were obviously exceptions to the trend and many unaffected by it. The group of society intellectuals known as 'The Souls' epitomised the reaction to the mindlessness of many late Victorian and Edwardian house parties or shooting weekends. For those outside the main stream of upper class life, those who were unable or chose not to be in London for the season, change in the country-house way of life must have been barely perceptible. That most unlikeable of Jane Austen's heroines, Fanny Price, was not alone in seeing London society as the solvent of traditional relationships and manners, and the country-side as the binding influence on virtue to achieve 'propriety, regularity, harmony'. Forster, in *Howard's End*, remarks:

> London was but a foretaste of this nomadic civilisation which is altering human nature so profoundly, and throws upon personal relations a stress greater than they have ever borne before. Under cosmopolitanism, if it comes, we shall receive no help from the earth. Trees and meadows and mountains will only be a spectacle and the binding force that they once exercised on character must be entrusted to Love alone.

There was little to disturb the even tenor of estate life, unless one was of the unfortunate number driven under by the agricultural depression of the 1870s. Mechanisation of agriculture extended only to steam ploughing and threshing on more prosperous farms, and farm labourer remained the most common occupation. The sense of permanence in rural life is well conveyed by Sebastian in *The Edwardians*, of a much more sensitive nature than his hedonistic and sociable mother:

> He felt that in the placid continuity of Chevron lay a vitality of an order different from the brilliant excitement of his mother's world. It came now to him as an audible hum. The whole community of the great house was humming at its work. . . . All was warmth and security, leisure and continuity. An order of things which appeared unchangeable to the mind of nineteen hundred and five.

And a very enjoyable order it was for those at the bell-pull end. National and local responsibilities there might have been, but government was then a much more leisurely and gentlemanly affair than now, allowing even ministers the leisure to enjoy weekend house parties without the fear of urgent recall, the interruption of the telephone, or boxes of papers to preclude joining the shooting party. Agents or factors generally looked after the administration of the estate, requiring the landowner's involvement on only major issues or investment. Gamekeepers ensured a ready supply of game for weekend or longer shooting parties, and hunting was perhaps the most cohesive and gregarious occupation in rural society. Fishing, cricket against the village team, croquet and tennis were the usual country-house sports, while hunt balls, subscription balls and frequent dinner parties filled the evenings.

These years were in many ways the Indian summer of the country house and its way of life. By the end of the period, both the justification of the aristocrat as an indispensable figure in national government or local administration had lost its validity, and the financial foundation upon which the class depended had begun to be seriously eroded with the introduction in 1894 of death duties, specifically intended to prevent the transfer of accumulated wealth from generation to generation. The wisdom of British gradualism and pragmatism is exemplified by the slow transfer of power and position which went on during the nineteenth and early twentieth centuries, as often as not inspired by liberal-minded landowners who realised the inevitability of a more modest role in the future Great Britain. Legislation to reduce the miseries of the Industrial Revolution might never have reached the statute book during Victoria's reign had it not been for the perseverance of Tory aristocrats. Less gratifying is the loss of art treasures and fine houses which began in a small way before, and accelerated after, the Great War. The loss and destruction continues, somewhat abated by government action in the wake of strong protest, but a major responsibility of the aristocracy has become the guardianship of much of what remains, carried out at no expense to the taxpayer, for a fraction of the cost were the government doing the job, and with all too little in the way of sensible fiscal arrangements regarding repairs to buildings. For this, the country has much cause for gratitude.

William Henry Fox Talbot had both the scientific background and the spare time conducive to his productive experiments which led to the invention of the calotype. Born the grandson of the Earl of Ilchester and Lord of the Manor at Lacock, he proved an outstanding scholar at Harrow and Trinity College, Cambridge. After three years in the Parliament which passed the Great Reform Bill, he devoted himself to capturing an image permanently through optics. The idea came to him while on honeymoon at Lake Como where he used a camera lucida and a camera obscura as optical aids to drawing. Success came in 1835 when the world's first negative was made, the subject being the window in the South Gallery at Lacock Abbey. Talbot also had the distinction of publishing the first book illustrated with photographs, *The Pencil of Nature*, which appeared in 1844. It was only to be expected that Talbot would choose the Abbey and those around him as his first subjects. They were chosen because they were convenient, rather than because he particularly wished to record such scenes. Yet his feeling for composition, in a medium that took decades to be accepted as an art form, is astonishing. In this example of Talbot's work, friends and estate workers pose in front of the stables at Lacock *c.*1844.

Science Museum, Lacock Abbey Collection

A group at the entrance to Lacock Abbey cloisters *c*.1843 beneath one of the console windows executed by John Chapman who worked for Henry VIII. The house was founded for Augustinian nuns in 1232 by the Countess of Salisbury in memory of her husband, William de Longespee. She became the first Abbess. Suppressed in 1539, Lacock was bought by Sir William Sharington who largely created the house as it is today, although a Gothick Hall was created in the mid-eighteenth century.

Lacock Abbey Collection

David Octavius Hill, RSA, was born in 1802, son of a
Perth publisher. Principally a landscape painter, he went
into collaboration with Robert Adamson in 1843 to
experiment with and develop the calotype because he
needed an *aide-mémoire* for an unusual painting. The
'Signing the Deed of Demission' compresses 470 Calvinist
divines into a canvas 11½ feet by 5 feet and
commemorates the schismatics who disrupted the Church
of Scotland in 1843 and formed the Free Church of
Scotland. The unsuccessful painting, which now hangs in
the Free Church Hall in Edinburgh, is largely forgotten,
but the 1,500 photographs produced by Hill and
Adamson in their five-year partnership are an invaluable
legacy. Besides taking portraits, they recorded landscapes
and anecdotal studies, and documented soldiers in the
capital. With Adamson's death in 1848, Hill abandoned
photography to return to his easel, although his
disruption picture was not finished until 1866.

This scene of Lord Cockburn and his family at Bonaly
Tower includes Hill, who is standing to the left of the
staircase behind two of Lord Cockburn's seated
daughters. Lord Cockburn is the gentleman on the right,
hat in hand, and the seated gentleman on the left is the
sculptor John Henning (1771–1851) who sculpted Mrs
Siddons and Princess Charlotte of Wales. Lady Cockburn
is seated at the foot of the stairs. Bonaly was the retreat
of Lord Cockburn in his retirement. Judge, recorder of
his times and namesake of Edinburgh's oldest amenity
society, Lord Cockburn (1779–1854) was appointed
solicitor general for Scotland by the Grey ministry of
1830. After his death, Thomas Carlyle wrote of him as
having 'rustic Scottish sense, sincerity and humour'.
Bonaly Tower, in the lea of the Pentland Hills, was
designed in 1836 by Playfair, one of the architects of the
Scottish revival movement of which William Burn was
the leading exponent. Now converted into flats, the
tower successfully recaptures much of the flavour of a
tower-house.

University of Glasgow

Nevil Story-Maskelyne (1823–1911) was another pioneer of photographic development although twenty-three years junior to Fox Talbot. The two men met in London in 1847, the older man's distant politeness turning to affability as Story-Maskelyne disclosed his original thoughts on the problem of preventing the solarisation of bright objects. His contribution might have been greater had his father not pressed him to discard his scientific inclinations in favour of a career at the Bar. He bowed to his father's directives: 'My camera shall be my sole scientific companion, yet not a scientific one, I shall only make it an artistic one.' In fact he did later relinquish his legal studies to become lecturer in mineralogy at Oxford and Keeper of Minerals at the British Museum.

His father's home was Basset Down House in Wiltshire, a square Georgian building, not far from Charlton Park near Malmesbury, seat of the Howards. It was on a visit there that Story-Maskelyne took this picture of the two sons of the Earl of Suffolk c.1855. Standing is the eldest son, Henry Charles, Viscount Andover (1833–98) who was a keen sportsman and writer on horse racing and riding, and became M.P. for Malmesbury. The other, Greville Theophilus, became a barrister and married Lady Townshend, who re-married Gen. Rt Hon. Sir Redvers Buller after Greville's death.

By courtesy of N.A. Foster

Tonge Hall near Middleton, in Lancashire, was a residence appropriate in size for the prosperous yeoman farmer or small landowner. The date on the photograph is 1894, but it must have been taken long before that date. Until 1890 it was tenanted by a farmer and then became unoccupied, at about the time when the hall was bought by Mr Asheton Tonge of Alderley. Why he allowed the hall to fall into disrepair is unknown, but in 1906 he offered it as a gift to the town of Middleton for use as a museum. In the spirit of philistinism that characterised the rejection of Mentmore, the council declined the donation. Before the hall became untenanted, a small porch was built over the door to the left of the picture so, with the ladies' garments as further evidence, the date is probably nearer the 1870s. The hall probably dates from the latter part of the sixteenth century. The continuous repetition of quatrefoils broken only by the shallow coves which mark the first floor and eaves is unusual and gives a rich ornamental appearance. Stone flags covered the floor of the great hall which had an unconventionally sited fireplace where the screen should have been. The rather delicate plough on the left and the harrow on the right are noteworthy.

Middleton Public Libraries

The Garrard family and gardener at Athelington Hall
c.1862. The small country house owned by the lesser
squire or farmer was obviously much more common
than the grand mansion set in hundreds of acres of
parkland, particularly in East Anglia. Naturally the estate
that supported the house was smaller too, but the
importance of this group of yeomen farmers is reflected
in 39% of England being composed of estates of 1,000
acres or less in the 1880s, notwithstanding the enormous
estates of the aristocracy. Originally moated, this early
seventeenth-century hall was situated near Eye, Suffolk.

Suffolk Photographic Survey

Welbeck Abbey came to the dukes of Portland by marriage in 1734. In common with Newstead (to become the home of Lord Byron) and Rufford, it had been a monastery amidst Sherwood Forest until the Dissolution under Henry VIII. In the late seventeenth century, the Duke of Kingston enclosed 1,270 of the 100,000 acres of the forest to form Thoresby Park, and a few years later the Duke of Newcastle followed suit, enclosing over 2,500 acres to form Clumber Park. By 1779, the Crown retained only 1,500 acres and much of the enclosed land had been landscaped by the new owners. Repton was responsible for modifying some of Welbeck's 3,000 acres, creating a lake that has since been enlarged to three miles in length. The earliest surviving records of construction pertain to the riding house and stables by Huntingdon Smythson, who worked with his father,

John, on the extraordinary gallery at nearby Bolsover. By 1734, Welbeck was ostensibly of comparable size, and ugliness, to the house seen here, but much of the work on the house in Victorian times was underground, providing an unrivalled example of the use of mining techniques in domestic architecture.

George Washington Wilson Collection, Aberdeen University

The 5th Duke of Portland (1800–79) lived an extraordinary life, even for an age given to eccentric conduct. He was described by Lady Ottoline Morrell, step-sister of the 6th Duke, as a 'lonely, self-isolated man'. Although he confined himself to four or five rooms, communicating through in and out letterboxes, he devoted himself to making Welbeck a home for sumptuous entertainment – underground. He never wished to be seen by anyone, dismissing servants whom he encountered and often walking at night. When it was vital for him to visit London, he would use a $1\frac{1}{4}$-mile tunnel from the Holbeck entrance to the south gate of Worksop Manor, travelling in a black carriage with drawn blinds. Yet he was concerned for the welfare of his workmen, and it has been suggested that local unemployment may have encouraged him to undertake these extraordinary works; each of the 500 masons received a donkey and an umbrella when he began work to make travelling through the park more comfortable. A skating rink was built for his staff – although its use was obligatory. Fifteen miles of tunnel connected a suite of library rooms, a billiard room capable of holding six tables, a ballroom for 2,000 guests and a long conservatory with glass roof. The house has not been a home since 1932; it has been used as an Army College. This is the approach to the tunnel with one of over forty lodges around the circumference of the park.

George Washington Wilson, University of Aberdeen

Croquet beneath the ha-ha at Otterburn Tower in
Northumberland, which was mostly built in the second
half of the eighteenth century in castellated form around
a medieval tower-house. The ha-ha was a device
invented in the previous century by Charles Bridgeman
with the dual purpose of keeping deer and other animals
out of the formal gardens and to enhance the impression
of the house when seen from a distance.

Northumberland County Record Office

Home of the dukes of Argyll, Inverary Castle dates from the mid-eighteenth century and was the work of Roger Morris, who had previously designed Clearwell Castle in Gloucestershire. Work began in 1743 with the Adam family as contractors, and proceeded during the second Jacobite rebellion, a whole village being removed to make way for the castle (as happened at Stowe, Nuneham Courtenay and Milton Abbas). Morris' design was one of the first executed according to the principles of the Gothic revival, and this photograph shows the castle before the disastrous fire of 1877 destroyed the central 70-foot tower and upper floors. Dr Johnson had remarked that the castle would have looked better with another storey and after the fire it was given one. Anthony Salvin was commissioned to remodel Inverary and he re-designed the tower as the Armoury Hall, added a floor and built conical roofs on the corner towers. In 1799, a French professor of geology, Faujas St-Fond, published an account of his *Travels in England, Scotland and the Hebrides* during which he visited Inverary Castle. Although his journey was made several decades before Victoria acceded to the throne, it is unlikely that much more than mealtimes would have altered:

> We remained three whole days in this delightful retreat, devoting the mornings to natural history and the evenings to music and conversation. . . . The manner in which we spent our time at Inverary Castle was extremely agreeable.

Each person rose at any hour he pleased in the morning. Some took a ride, others went to the chace. I rose with the sun and proceeded to examine the natural history of the environs. . . . At ten o'clock a bell summoned us to breakfast: we then repaired to a large room. Here we found several breakfast tables, covered with tea, coffee, excellent cream, and everything the appetite could desire, surrounded with bouquets of flowers, newspapers and books. There were, besides, in this room, a billiard table, a piano-forte, and other musical instruments. After breakfast, some walked in the parks, others amused themselves with reading and music, or returned to their apartments. . . . At half past four, the dinner bell was rung, and we went to the dining room, where we always found a table of twenty-five or thirty covers.

Royal Commission on the Ancient and Historical Monuments of Scotland

Haddo House in Aberdeenshire was planned in 1731 by
William Adam, father of the better-known brothers. It
was built for the 2nd Earl of Aberdeen to replace the
House of Kellie, which had been the home of the
Gordons of Methlick for centuries. The architect of the
chapel was G.E. Street (who also designed the chapel and
huge library at nearby Dunecht and the Law Courts in
the Strand) and the east window is by Burne-Jones. Not
all the earls of Aberdeen have admired their seat – the
4th Earl, who was to become Prime Minister, was
appalled by the gaunt building when he returned to take
up his inheritance at the age of twenty after an absence
of many years. Creating an estate of prosperity and
beauty became his main source of pleasure, entailing the
planting of 14 million trees and the construction of many
granite-built farm buildings for the 900 farms on the estate.

George Washington Wilson Collection, Aberdeen University

Glenlochy House, Perthshire, owes something in its design to the ideals behind the *cottage ornée*. The artificial quest for a Rousseauesque Arcadianism, somewhat vulgarised by the whimsical eccentricities of Marie Antoinette and her dairy, led to the creation of modest residences in which the keynote was simplicity. No sacrifice of comfort was made, but ornamentation should be subdued and serve to emphasise the building's rustic nature or pretensions. (The Royal Lodge in Windsor Park, designed by Nash for George IV, was the idea taken to a ludicrous conclusion.)

By courtesy of the Earl of Cawdor

Few of the architectural studies taken by George Washington Wilson or his employees included people. This pleasing exception depicts Flichity House in Strath Nairn, ten miles south of Inverness.

George Washington Wilson Collection, Aberdeen University

The games table at Brocket Hall in July 1898 with Lord Mount-Stephen, seated in the foreground, Lady Mount-Stephen, standing on the left, Lady Mary Trefusis to her right, and Victoria Mary, Duchess of York seated in the centre. It was at Brocket and on the banks of the nearby River Lee that William Lamb, 2nd Viscount Melbourne and future Prime Minister, spent his childhood. The connection with Melbourne Hall had been established by Matthew Lamb, William's grandfather, who had married Charlotte Coke, heiress of Melbourne Hall. He had bought Brocket in 1746.

William Lamb married the tempestuous Lady Caroline Ponsonby and they spent their honeymoon at Brocket — it was then rare for a couple to do otherwise than spend their honeymoon at home. The house was to be the scene of some of Lady Caroline's unbridled outbursts and eccentricities. In 1841, Brocket was graced by a visit from Queen Victoria during a tour of Whig houses to demonstrate her confidence in government ministers. Lord Melbourne spent most of the last eighteen months of his life at Brocket, dying in 1848. Brocket passed to the 6th Earl Cowper through Lady Cowper, William's sister, and was later sold to Lord Mount-Stephen.

Reproduced by gracious permission of Her Majesty the Queen

The picture gallery at Welbeck Abbey. The debt owed by the nation to the collecting activities of the aristocracy is enormous. Of course magnanimous and altruistic instincts played little part in their motivation, but the fact remains that were it not for their passion for accumulating art treasures, we would not have the magnificent heritage we enjoy. (Perhaps the most notable exception to this self-interest was the Bowes Museum, consciously created by John and Josephine Bowes, who lived at Streatlam Castle and Gibside. Their astonishingly diverse collection was built up between the 1840s and 1870s with public exhibition in mind and came to be housed in the huge museum at Barnard Castle, opened in 1892.)

The interest in collecting was often created by the customary grand tour which was designed to complete a young gentleman's formal education. The revival of interest in the classical past with the discoveries of Pompeii and Herculaneum gave a strong Middle Eastern bias to tours arranged for the more serious and cultured. Many of the antiquities picked up on the way are now in the British Museum and the bulk of the Egyptian collection in the Gulbenkian Museum at Durham University was acquired by the 4th Duke of Northumberland. Patronage of living artists, however, was uncommon, portrait commissions of horses and humans apart. The support given by the 4th Duke of Richmond to Canaletto or that of the Earl of Egremont for Turner at Petworth was exceptional. Dutch, French and Italian paintings were the almost exclusive interests of collectors.

George Washington Wilson, King's College, Aberdeen

Founded during the reign of King Stephen, the priory situated in the manor of Beechwood, near Flamstead in Hertfordshire, was dissolved by Henry VIII in 1537. By the late seventeenth century the manor was owned by the Sebright family, who lived there until the early years of this century. The house is now a preparatory school. The family had formerly lived at Besford Court in Worcestershire, and established the Sebright School at Wolverley in the same county. The paternal tradition continued in Hertfordshire: Sir John Sebright, who lived at Beechwood Park when Victoria came to the throne, endowed a school and built a row of almshouses for sixteen paupers in Flamstead. Built during the reign of William III with rainheads dated 1702, the house retains one room with wide fireplace dating from the early sixteenth century, if not before. This photograph shows the large hall which was an open courtyard until 1854 when Sir Thomas Sebright, the 8th Baronet, enclosed it. Top-lit and decorated in Italian Renaissance manner by Barbetti, a Florentine carver, the hall is surrounded at first-floor level by a gallery, although most of the former window openings have been blocked.

Luton Museum

The earliest known rules for the game of billiards were printed in 1650 and it was during the seventeenth century that the first tables were installed in country houses. However, it was not until the late eighteenth and early nineteenth centuries that the game became really fashionable. As the nineteenth century progressed, the game was increasingly combined with the burgeoning habit of smoking, and billiard and smoking rooms tended to be adjacent. As a result, the game became something of a male preserve, although the 6th Duke and Duchess of Buccleuch played billiards every day until the end of their married life. This is the billiard room at Glenquoich Lodge, a shooting lodge above Loch Quoich in Inverness-shire, where King Edward VII was an occasional guest. It was built by the Rt Hon. Edward Ellice, M.P. for Coventry, and furnished in the simplest manner with cane-bottomed chairs and iron bedsteads. The great engineer, Joseph Mitchell, stayed there in 1850 as the only untitled guest in 'a large and fashionable company. . . . The gentlemen were early on the mountain side, while the ladies occupied themselves in boating, driving, walking, writing, sketching and quiet gossip.'

George Washington Wilson Collection, Aberdeen University

The ground-floor billiard room in the south-east wing of Mentmore, with Baroness Meyer de Rothschild and her daughter, Hannah, later Lady Rosebery, standing by the table. The photograph was taken before her marriage to the 5th Earl of Rosebery in 1878, as Baroness Meyer died the year before it. The 5th Earl became Prime Minister after Gladstone in 1894 and was created Viscount Mentmore in 1911. Lady Rosebery died in 1890. Built in 1852–4, the house was designed for Baron Meyer Amschel de Rothschild by Sir Joseph Paxton and his son-in-law G.H. Stokes. The design was inspired by Wollaton Hall, Nottingham, Smythson's Elizabethan mansion for the Willoughby family. Both were built of Ancaster stone with solid square angle towers and a huge central hall. Mentmore was one of the first Victorian country houses to incorporate hot water heating and artificial ventilation throughout. The black and white marble chimney piece in the Great Hall came from Rubens' house in Antwerp. The opportunity to acquire the house and its exceptional contents for the nation was lost in 1978 through government indifference and a betrayal of the ideals behind the establishment of the Land Fund.

By courtesy of Lord Rosebery

The 9th Countess of Southesk at her writing desk at Kinnaird Castle, Angus, in 1898. The Earl, 6th *de facto* and 9th *de jure*, married Lady Susan Murray, daughter of the 6th Earl of Dunmore, in 1860, five years after obtaining an Act of Parliament reversing the attainder of 1715 on the 5th Earl for his part in the Jacobite rebellion. The 9th Earl was a man of refined tastes, not only transforming Kinnaird from a castellated mansion with square centre tower and one at each corner into a *château*, but amassing a large collection of antique gems, old masters, books, and about 150 cylinders of Assyrian, Hittite, Babylonian, Persian and Accadian origin. Some of these and most of the library were destroyed in a serious fire in 1921, but most of the pictures were saved. For his exploration of the remoter parts of the Rockies he was made a fellow of the Geographical Society.

Royal Commission on the Ancient Monuments of Scotland, by courtesy of the Earl of Southesk

The panelled and pilastered drawing room of Loton Park near Alderbury, Shropshire, in the 1890s, with the clutter typical of the period, including birdcage. The lady is thought to be Lady Leighton. She was to become one of the first female Masters of Foxhounds during the absence of her husband, Sir Baldwin Leighton, for the duration of the Boer War. The house was built in the 1670s.

By courtesy of Sir Michael Leighton

Sir James Kitson (1835–1911) in his study at Gledhow Hall, Leeds. At the age of 19 he was put in charge of his father's Monkbridge ironworks, and his life was devoted to engineering until his late fifties, when he was elected Liberal member for Colne Valley. To contest the seat, he resigned his presidency of the Iron and Steel Institute. He was Lord Mayor of Leeds and raised to the Peerage as Baron Airedale in 1907. A contemporary wrote of him in that year:

> Everything about James Kitson spells solidity and endurance – from the great offices of Kitson & Co in the centre of town to the square grey hall outside on the hilltop whence he looks out over the green countryside westwards. There he leads a simple and patriarchal life amongst his children. There he entertains . . . the leading men of his day, never permitting his life to be narrowed by business or allowing the pressure of affairs to eclipse the natural humanity of his kindly nature.

Being a prominent industrialist, and a local and national politician with his constituency nearby, it was inevitable that entertaining on a considerable scale was a frequent duty for James Kitson. The account books for Gledhow are filled with entries for parties for workers from the Colne Valley, dinner parties when Gladstone, Rosebery, Campbell-Bannerman or Asquith stayed at the hall, garden parties for employees from the works, Liberal Party functions and balls in connection with the Leeds Triennial Festival. For example, on 6 July 1889, sixty

foremen from the Monkbridge and Airedale works consumed 52lb salmon, 208 bread buns, 20 chickens, 2 hams, beef sirloin, 7 tongues, veal and ham pies, 60lb strawberries, 60lb cherries, 12 cakes and cheese – cost £14 18s. 3d. The largest recorded gathering was in 1907 when 1,200 members of the Ancient Order of Foresters were given afternoon tea at a cost of 1s. 6d. a head.

Leeds City Archives

The library at Invergarry House, near Fort Augustus, a mansion erected in 1868–9 from designs by David Bryce, William Burn's talented assistant and later partner. Libraries, as important separate rooms, were rare until the eighteenth century. Then used as the main recreation room during the daytime, they often included collections of prints, paintings and even a billiard table if a separate room had not been provided for that game. In Victorian times, the eighteenth-century ideal of the cultivated gentleman seeking knowledge and enlightenment waned, and libraries sometimes suffered as a result. Libraries were often there to impress and the books in them neglected by the occupants of the house. (Their size, however, did not diminish. The library built in the 1880s for the Earl of Crawford and Balcarres at Dunecht measured 120 feet by 27 feet, with two galleries above, off which were two reading rooms, 24 feet by 16 feet.)

George Washington Wilson Collection, Aberdeen University

Right: Even photographs of servants rarely showed them at work, or pretending that they were, so this view of the kitchen at Kinnaird Castle in Angus is unusual. Victorian kitchens shone with polished brass and copper, the metals from which most utensils were made. The single gas mantel can hardly have been adequate for the room but standards of illumination have doubtless changed. Kinnaird Castle was then and still is the seat of the Earl of Southesk, a title granted by Charles I at the same time as that of the Earl of Northesk, to two brothers in the Carnegie family.

Royal Commission on the Ancient and Historical Monuments of Scotland, by courtesy of the Earl of Southesk

Chess in the Barons' Hall of the old Nevill stronghold at Raby Castle. It was hardly an appropriate room for an intimate game – even in medieval times it was capable of holding the 700 Knights of Raby – and another 50 feet were added in the 1840s under the guidance of William Burn. It was during the remodelling that the room was given its massive hammer-beam roof. The identity of the players is unknown but it is fairly evident who was the more confident of victory. All that is known is that the contest took place during the time of Harry, the 4th and last Duke of Cleveland who made Raby a gathering place for politicians, writers and artists. He died in 1891.

By courtesy of Lord Barnard

Right: The kitchen at Lathom House near Ormskirk in Lancashire, *c.*1880. In common with sanitary engineering, kitchen equipment underwent a major change during the nineteenth century. Sophisticated cast-iron ranges and warming cupboards helped to make both cooking and serving food easier. Warming cupboards, the equivalent of today's hot plates and trolleys, were particularly necessary in Victorian houses, which were generally designed to keep kitchen smells far removed from the dining room. On the right may be seen the gearing for the spit which appears to be positioned to allow the smoke and draught in the chimney to provide the power. Such an arrangement was not uncommon and the mechanism survives and may be seen at Saltram House and Lankydrock, for example. Lathom House was built for Sir Thomas Bootle to the designs of Giacomo Leoni, work taking five years, from 1725 to 1730. Leoni was instrumental in propagating the ideas of Palladio in England and his greatest contributions to our heritage were Clandon Park in Surrey, home of the Onslow family, the south front at Lyme Hall in Cheshire and Moor Park in Hertfordshire.

National Monuments Record

Breakfasting in the library at Ickworth in Suffolk c.1880. A much more substantial affair in Victorian times than now, breakfast was an informal meal when the family was without guests, and its time was flexible in as much as it was customary for the hot dishes to be served in silver entrée dishes, kept warm by burners on a sideboard.

When guests were staying, it became a more formal occasion at which plans for the day could be discussed. One may generalise by saying that the degree of formality and organisation of entertainment diminished as the Victorian era neared its end. In the early years of Victoria's reign it would have been unthinkable for a host to be out shooting when guests for a house party arrived; in Edwardian times, much greater laxity in etiquette was evident. Dinner alone remained an unbendingly formal occasion, whether guests were staying or not.

Ickworth was the extraordinary creation of the equally extraordinary 4th Earl of Bristol (known as the Earl-Bishop since he held the profitable bishopric of Derry), who devoted little time to his ecclesiastical duties and far more to his passion for collecting works of art. This entailed prolonged absence from his diocese while travelling around Europe, in particular Germany and Italy. The colossal scale of Ickworth was intended to house his treasures, many of which were sadly lost after building had been commenced when Napoleon invaded Italy in 1798. The Bishop was imprisoned in Milan for nine months and his collection confiscated. He never saw the progress made on Ickworth for he died in 1803 after supervising its design and construction by letter for nine years. Ickworth was regarded as having been the work of Francis Sandys but it is now thought that the mansion was built to the designs of an Italian architect, Mario Asprucci the younger, whose father was curator of the Borghese collections in Rome. The role of Francis Sandys and his brother, the Rev. Joseph, has been relegated to that of superintendence of construction. It was left to the 5th Earl to complete his father's scheme, the family finally moving into the mansion in 1829. The library is the largest of the state rooms in the rotunda.

The National Trust

Tea on the lawn at Knole near Sevenoaks in Kent on 26
August 1899, with Prince Alexander of Teck standing
with thumb in pocket, the Duchess of York to his right,
Frank Dugdale in the straw boater, and Lady Eva
Dugdale seated on the extreme right. Prince Alexander
(1874–1957) was born at Kensington Palace, the son of
the Duke of Teck, had a distinguished military career,
attaining the rank of brigadier-general, and became the
first and last Earl of Athlone following his marriage in
1904 to H.R.H. Princess Alice, Countess of Athlone. He
served in the Matabele and Boer wars, was Governor-
General of South Africa from 1923–31, and became
personal A.D.C. to four monarchs, George V, Edward
VIII, George VI, and Queen Elizabeth II. Vita Sackville-
West, then aged seven, is seated on the ground. Knole
was the setting for Virginia Woolf's strange novel
Orlando and the basis for Chevron in Vita Sackville-
West's *The Edwardians*.

Tea on the lawn at Barton, a country house near Osborne on the Isle of Wight, on 4 August 1909. Seated round the table from left to right are George, Prince of Wales, Princess Victoria, Tsar Nicholas II, Queen Alexandra, King Edward VII, and Victoria Mary, Princess of Wales. Afternoon tea was made fashionable by Anna, Duchess of Bedford, and indirectly helped by the Earl of Sandwich, who had earlier created the idea of two slices of bread with filling to relieve his hunger at the gambling table. Afternoon tea on the lawn under the shade of ancestral oaks and cedars became one of the classic images of England at this time. Nicholas II was on an official visit and was received at Cowes on 2 August by Edward VII. The king met the Emperor of Russia aboard the Russian royal yacht *Standart* which was accompanied by two cruisers and two destroyers. The home and Atlantic fleets had been assembled for a Royal Naval Review on 31 July, and the Tsar was taken through the lines aboard the royal yacht *Victoria and Albert* on the 2nd, the bands playing the Russian national anthem. On 3 August the two monarchs watched the racing at Cowes, and on 4 August the Tsar visited Osborne College and House before taking tea at Barton Manor. The Tsar's children had tea at Osborne Cottage, home of Princess Henry of Battenburg, where they were joined by the royal entourage after tea at Barton was over. It was to be the last visit of the Russian royal family to England and did not pass without protest: Keir Hardie addressed a meeting, and 180 Bishops, Deans, members of Parliament, authors, professors and editors signed a letter to *The Times* reminding readers of the condition of political prisoners and exiles in Russia. *Plus ça change, plus c'est la même chose.* Barton Manor was owned by the warden and scholars of Winchester College from 1439–1853, when it was purchased by the Prince Consort to become part of the Osborne estate. The house was entirely rebuilt in Jacobean style, but great care was taken to preserve its character, incorporating lancet windows from the Augustinian oratory which had been founded on the site in 1275. Osborne was given to the nation by Edward VII in 1902, becoming a convalescent home for officers of both services, but Barton was obviously retained.

Reproduced by gracious permission of
Her Majesty The Queen

The Banqueting Hall at Naworth Castle near Brampton in Cumberland was the largest in the county. It was built during the sixteenth century and severely damaged during a fire in 1844. The roof, which was painted with fine portraits of the Saxon Kings of England, fell in and only the walls remained. Salvin restored the castle and was faithful to the old, introducing little. The strange heraldic beasts on either side of the fireplace are two of four oak figures which have been the subject of much controversy. Some believe them to have been brought from nearby Kirkoswald Castle by Lord William Howard, but the consensus of opinion seems to be that they are of Tudor origin, probably from the reign of Henry VII, and their heraldic significance suggests that they were made for Thomas Lord Dacre and intended to carry banners at tournaments. Naworth Castle has been converted into flats.

George Washington Wilson, King's College, Aberdeen

The dinner table at Goodwood House in July 1897, laid
for a Race-week repast, at which Edward VII would have
been present. The time of the meal had become rather
later during the nineteenth century; in the late
eighteenth century, dinner would be served at 4.30–5.00
and supper would follow at 10.00 or 11.00. Guests would
assemble in the drawing room, attired in full dress and
possibly decorations, to be led into the dining room by
their host and hostess. At Sandringham, Edward VII was
meticulous in his arrangements, making sure that an
equerry had informed the men of their partners and that
each lady should have the honour of being taken in by
her royal host. The meal would be served with elegance,
numerous footmen in attendance and the plate on
display. It became the custom for the ladies to retire to
the drawing room while the men remained to enjoy port
and cigars and conversation either unfit for the ladies'
sensibilities or of a political nature. Racing at Goodwood
began in 1801 under the aegis of the 3rd Duke of
Richmond, who was also largely responsible for the
creation of Goodwood House. Employing James Wyatt,
he had intended Goodwood to be an octagon with a
tower at each corner but, mercifully for his ancestors,
only three sides were completed by his death in 1806.

Reproduced by gracious permission of
Her Majesty The Queen

With slow photographic plates it was inevitable that interior scenes were rarely recorded. This dinner party was held at Brocket Hall in Hertfordshire in July 1898, and guests included the Duchess of York, wearing a dark dress and seated to the left of centre, and Lady Mary Trefusis, seated on the right. The host and hostess are Lord and Lady Mount-Stephen; he is seated, arms crossed, and Lady Mount-Stephen is on the extreme left. Lord Mount-Stephen was the epitome of the Victorian self-made man who was assimilated by the aristocracy, elevated to the peerage and later given the final approbation by receiving royalty. Born in 1829 in the village of Mortlach in the County of Banff, he was employed in drapery businesses in Aberdeen and London until 1851, when he emigrated to Canada. There he made a fortune from the manufacture of woollen goods, becoming President of the Bank of Montreal and the Canadian Pacific Railway. In the 1890s he returned to England to live, purchasing Brocket Hall from Earl Cowper, and in the year before this dinner had married his second wife, Georgina Tufnell, daughter of a commander in the Royal Navy. At the time of the dinner, the Duke of York was serving in the Royal Navy as commander of the cruiser *Crescent*. Lady Mary Trefusis was the daughter of Lord Clinton; she died in

1954, aged 92. Lord Mount-Stephen also reached the venerable age of 92, dying at Brocket in 1921, when the peerage became extinct.

The square red brick house by James Paine was begun about 1755 and not completed until 1780. It is now a ruin, but some items of decoration, such as overmantles, were removed for use at Melbourne Hall.

Reproduced by gracious permission of
Her Majesty The Queen

One of the entrances to Blair Castle, revealing a long
drive guarded by the lodge. The entrance and approach
to a country house became of great importance during
the eighteenth century with the burgeoning of theories
and treatises on the art of landscape gardening. The first
use of the term in print appears to have been in 1764
with the posthumous publication of *Works* by William
Shenstone: 'I have used the word landskip-gardiners,
because in pursuance of our present taste in gardening,
every good painter of landskip appears to me the most
proper designer.' Shenstone devoted his life and limited
wealth to beautifying the grounds at his home, the
Leasowes, near Halesowen, which became in Johnson's
words 'a place to be visited by travellers, and copied by
designers'. He particularly emphasised the need to
involve the mind during a walk in a garden – hence the
contemporary interest in creating ruins, urns, mock
temples, sculptures and inscriptions around the grounds.
First impressions were equally important, so the gates
should be imposing, and perhaps proclaim the lineage of
the owner by bearing his arms in iron. The length of the
drive was naturally some indication of the size of the
grounds.

Perth Museum

Although construction of country houses naturally went on throughout the Victorian and Edwardian eras, particularly by wealthy industrialists, photographs showing any facet of their creation are surprisingly rare. This scene shows the construction of the drive for Waddesdon Manor. Baron Ferdinand de Rothschild (1839–98) bought Waddesdon and Winchendon estates from the 7th Duke of Marlborough in 1874, and set about levelling and planting Lodge Hill on which the house was to stand. The house was designed by a French architect, Gabriel Hippolyte Destailleur, and incorporated features borrowed from *châteaux* along the Loire. To carry the Bath stone up the hillside, a tramway was constructed with steam haulage over the lower section and horses over the upper part. The horses were powerful Percheron mares specially imported from Normandy, and 16 were needed to haul the larger mature trees which were planted on the bare hillside. Baron Ferdinand became a member of the first County Council and M.P. for Aylesbury. Visitors and guests at Waddesdon included Queen Victoria, King Edward VII, Guy de Maupassant, Robert Browning, Lord Rosebery, Lloyd George and Sir Winston Churchill.

The National Trust

Left: The Dent family in the grounds of Barton Court, a house between Christchurch and Lymington in Hampshire.

By courtesy of the Earl of Harrowby

Below left: Horse-drawn mower at Euston Hall, taken before the disastrous fire of 1902 devastated the south and west wings, to the left and centre respectively in the photograph. Mercifully, the exceptional collection of Stuart portraits was removed before they were destroyed by flames – as John Evelyn, the diarist, put it, the whole house was 'fill'd from one end to the other with lords, ladys and gallants'.

After the fire, the hall was rebuilt on the same plan, but in 1952 the overheads and maintenance costs necessitated the demolition of the south and most of the west wing, retaining all the original rooms which had survived the fire. Work on the original house began in 1666 at the behest of one of the leading politicians of the time, the Earl of Arlington, who was a member of the 'cabal' then in power. It was completed by 1671 when John Evelyn stayed for a fortnight and supervised the planting of trees. William Kent was primarily responsible for the grounds, although minor modifications were carried out by Capability Brown in the later eighteenth century. Like Vanbrugh, Kent began his career in a different profession, producing inferior paintings and sculpture before he found his *métier*. Trained as a coach-painter in Hull, Kent was tactfully dissuaded from taking a personal hand in the decoration of his more ambitious designs. Walpole described him as the 'father of modern gardening', and his work may be said to exemplify the tenets set out in Pope's *Epistle to the Earl of Burlington*.

National Monuments Record

The garden at Gordon Castle, Morayshire, in the late nineteenth century.

The formal and fussy nature of the mid-Victorian garden required a large staff of gardeners. The Victorian era saw a return to classical and geometric layouts incorporating Italian-style ornaments, garden furniture and elaborate waterworks. The demands made on the kitchen garden also grew with the larger and more frequent house-parties made possible by the railways. At Knole, the pleasure gardens and four acres of walled kitchen garden kept twenty men and a head gardener busy. From the 1880s, the gardeners might be augmented by the ladies of the house who began to take an active, rather than appreciative, interest in the garden, encouraged by the example of Gertrude Jekyll who, with William Robinson, dominated the Edwardian reaction to Victorian formality.

Royal Commission on the Ancient and Historical Monuments of Scotland

The lake, boathouse and peddle-driven paddleboat, at Luton Hoo in 1885. While Adam was working on the house, Lancelot Brown was landscaping and enlarging the park from 300 acres to 1,200. He dammed the River Lea to create two lakes, the larger of which covers 60 acres and is nearly a quarter of a mile long. The beauty of the grounds remains, but Adam's house, acknowledged as magnificent by the critical Dr Johnson, was almost totally destroyed by fire in 1843. The library, considered by Adam to have been his *chef d'oeuvre* both in point of elegance and contrivance, held 30,000 volumes and was regarded as second only to Blenheim.

Luton Museum

The tropical corridor at Floors Castle in Roxburghshire. Although conservatories were a late Georgian invention, it was not until the early Victorian years that iron technology became sufficiently developed to enable large and elaborate structures to be erected. Joseph Paxton gave impetus to the use of glass and iron in the huge conservatories he designed and built at Chatsworth in 1836–40 and at Capesthorne a few years later. Sadly, both were demolished in the 1920s. Large conservatories were not intended solely for growing exotic plants. Use was made of them during parties, sometimes by hanging Chinese lanterns amongst the foliage. Rivalry grew up between some landowners over their success in growing foreign specimens, sent home or brought to England by such men as Stamford Raffles, who took a keen interest in recording the flora of territories under his administration. The owner of Flitwick Manor in Bedfordshire proudly recorded that the grape season extended from April to January, and that the 'fire of the peach house is lighted at the end of January, which produces fruit by the end of May. the fig house is heated at the same time, securing crops in succession from June to December.'

George Washington Wilson Collection, Aberdeen University

In 1896, the 1st Duke of Westminster commissioned Sir Arthur Heywood to construct a 15 inch gauge railway on his estate at Eaton Hall in Cheshire. Sir Arthur (1849–1916) was the grandson of a Manchester banker, and after being the first person to take a first in Applied Science at Cambridge, settled down in the role of amateur engineer at his Derbyshire home. He set about perfecting the idea of the 15 inch gauge railway for estate work or traffic levels of only 5,000 tons a year. The Duke of Westminster was his first and only customer. The line ran for three and three-quarter miles from the hall to Balderton exchange sidings on the Wrexham–Chester line, with a branch to the brickyard and store yard. The railway had two engines and one is seen here in December 1909 at what appears to be the start of a day's shooting or riding. Driver Wilde kept a list of distinguished passengers and these included the Duchess of Teck, King Edward VII and Queen Alexandra, King Alfonso of Spain and Winston Churchill. The main traffic was bringing coal to the hall but the railway was even used for staff occasions, such as the Retainers' Ball, held every Christmas in the hall, when the staff arrived and left by train. Although Sir Arthur's ideas did not receive wider acceptance, two other houses were served by specially built railways: Belvoir Castle by a horse-drawn tramway which actually entered the castle basement, constructed in 1815; and Sand Hutton in Yorkshire, where an 18 inch gauge line was built by Sir Robert Walker in 1920. He took a particular interest and pride in the line, which closed in 1932, soon after his death. The Eaton Hall Railway survived until 1946.

Radio Times Hulton Picture Library

Above right: A request to a visitor for the ceremony of planting a tree has always been a token of esteem by the host. George, Prince of Wales, is seen here after planting a tree at Orwell in the parish of Nacton, Suffolk. Named after the nearby River Orwell, the hall used to be the home of Admiral Vernon, who captured Porto Bello from the Spaniards with six ships and the loss of only seven men. He was known as 'Old Grog' for his introduction of the rum ration. A century later it was the seat of George Tomline of Suffolk. The house is now a boy's preparatory school.

Reproduced by gracious permission of Her Majesty The Queen

It was naturally customary to record on film for posterity such occasions as the visit of royalty. This group is pictured outside Gwydyr, Caernarvonshire, in April 1899. From left to right: Lord Lincolnshire, Lord Boston, Marjorie, Lady Carrington, Ronald Moncrieffe, Mrs Cornwallis West (seated), Lady Lincolnshire, the Duchess and Duke of York (later King George V), General Swaine, Lady Magdalen Bulkeley (seated, in fur capes), Lady Boston, Miss Cornwallis West, the Hon. Derek Keppel (behind Lady Boston), Col Cornwallis West, Col Wynne Finch and Sir Richard Bulkeley. Lord Lincolnshire, Charles Wynn-Carrington (1843–1928), was a close friend of Edward VII who had refused to leave him behind when he went on his Indian tour in 1875, despite Queen Victoria's disapproval. Disraeli placated the Queen and assured her that he would caution Carrington 'against larks'. Later he was made Governor of New South Wales and after his return to England given a seat in the cabinet. Lord Boston enjoyed livings in Anglesey. The Hon. Derek Keppel, son of the 7th Earl of Albemarle, held various positions in the royal household. Col Wynne Finch was a local landowner and former colonel in the Scots Guards. Sir Richard Bulkeley was Lord Lieutenant of Anglesey where he owned an estate – Plas Meigan.

Reproduced by gracious permission of Her Majesty The Queen

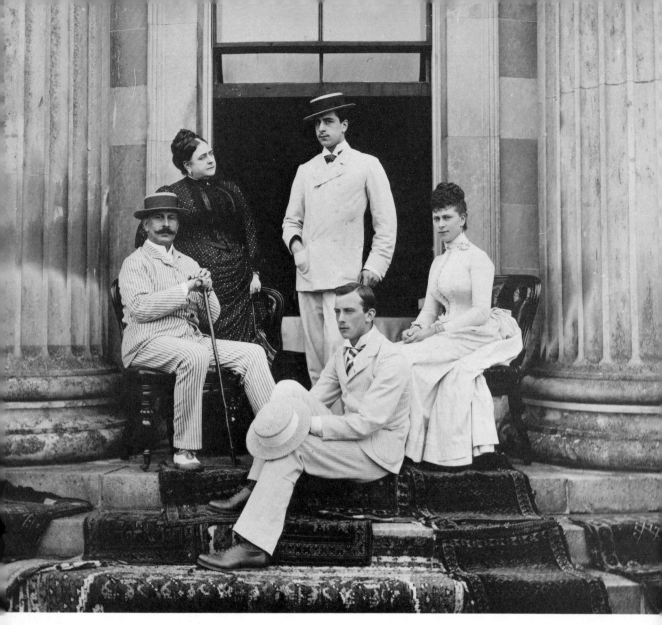

A group on the steps of Luton Hoo, Bedfordshire on 9 August 1888. On the left are the Duke and Duchess of Teck, and their three children, Prince Adolphus of Teck (standing), Prince Francis of Teck, and Princess May, then aged 21. The title was inherited by the House of Württemburg in the fourteenth century. The Duke served in the Franco-Italian campaign, was decorated for distinguished services at the Battle of Solferino in 1859, and married the grand daughter of George III, H.R.H. Mary Adelaide of Cambridge, Princess of Great Britain and Ireland, in 1866. He subsequently served in the British army which suppressed the nationalist revolt in Egypt in 1881–2. The Duchess of Teck was born at the viceregal palace in Hanover in 1833, and after their marriage the Duke and Duchess lived in London, first in Kensington Palace and then at White Lodge, Richmond Park. Her brother, the 2nd Duke of Cambridge, had ensured the extinction of the title by marrying a popular actress in contravention of the Royal Marriage Act of 1772, making even his children born within wedlock illegitimate. Prince Adolphus succeeded to the title on the death of his father in 1900 but relinquished it and the style of Highness in 1917, being created Marquess of Cambridge. He became personal A.D.C. to King George V and died in 1927. His brother, Prince Francis, served in the Boer War and died unmarried at the young age of 40.

Luton Museum

Below Left to right, standing: Lord Gordon Lennox, Count Menedorff, Lady Eva Greville, H.R.H. The Prince of Wales, Frances Countess of Warwick, H.R.H. The Duchess of York, Duchess of Teck. Left to right, sitting: Prince Francis of Teck, Lady Lister Kaye, Earl of Warwick, Lady Lillian Wemyss, Count Soveral.

At the age of three, in 1864, Frances Evelyn Maynard inherited nearly 14,000 acres, worth over £20,000 a year in rents alone, and Easton Lodge, a huge mock-Elizabethan mansion near Dunmow in Essex. In 1881 she married Lord Brooke, heir to the 4th Earl of Warwick. It was not long before frustration with their divergent interests and dispositions led Lady Brooke to seek distractions from what she regarded as the tedium of sporting house-parties. After becoming mistress to a number of men, Lady Brooke was taken up by the Prince of Wales following his help in trying to prevent a scandal of her creation in coming to court. He became a regular visitor to Easton Lodge, and Lord and Lady Brooke to Sandringham. This photograph is of a visit in late October 1891 to Easton Lodge which was curtailed by news of a fire at Sandringham on 1 November. The following day the Prince of Wales drove to Elsenham station and took a train to Sandringham where he found the report of the damage so exaggerated that he returned to London the same day, attending a performance of *Joan of Arc* at the Gaiety Theatre with the Duke of Clarence and Prince George that evening. The programme at Easton on such occasions began with breakfast at 10.00.

When the many silver dishes were empty, the men would depart to begin their shooting, leaving the ladies to amuse themselves with conversation or letter writing. Luncheon was served 'in the field', obliging the ladies to don suitable garments and irritating the men by interrupting their sport. Conversation at tea time was enlivened, or made insufferable, by a shot-by-shot report. Yet another change of clothes took the ladies to dinner. It was the hours between tea and dinner that Lady Brooke found most irksome, etiquette insisting that guests and host remain in their rooms until summoned to dinner. Lady Brooke was naturally able to choose company that could be expected to relieve the boredom when organising parties in her own home. On this occasion she secured the man recognised as being 'the most popular in London', the Marquis de Soveral, the Portuguese Minister. Nicknamed the 'Blue Monkey' because of his animated manner, blue-black hair and dark complexion, Frederick Ponsonby remarked of him that 'without being exactly witty his conversation was always sparkling and amusing'. Lady Brooke became a dedicated socialist, allowing the T.U.C. the use of Easton Lodge during her later years and leaving it to the Congress on her death. It was later demolished. It was her political views that led to an estrangement between Lady Brooke and the Prince of Wales, although they remained platonic friends.

Essex Record Office

The imposing Duchess of Teck is led downstairs by Sir Humphrey de Trafford at Trafford Park in October 1887. They are followed by Princess May of Teck and Lord Greenock, and Lady de Trafford with the Duke of Teck. Sir Humphrey de Trafford was descended from one of the oldest families in the country, his pedigree commencing with Randolphus de Trafford who flourished at the time of King Canute c.1030. The unbroken male succession was seated in the parish of Eccles from that time and their home became known as Trafford Park. The house, of freestone with a semicircular front divided by columns, was demolished in 1937. Formerly in the Royal Dragoons, Sir Humphrey married the elder sister of the 17th Earl of Shrewsbury. Lord Greenock was son of the Earl of Cathcart, and after a career in the Scots Guards died unmarried in a London nursing home in 1911.

Reproduced by gracious permission of
Her Majesty The Queen

Fun and frivolity are rarely captured in old photographs, primarily because of the long exposures necessary, but also because most photographs were taken to record special occasions, which were almost without exception formal in nature. So this picture of Lord Berkeley Paget, Lord Alexander Paget, the Earl of Uxbridge, and a mock-indignant Captain Billington at Plas Newydd is of particular interest. Lord Berkeley Paget (1844–1913) was the fourth son and Lord Alexander Paget (1839–96) the third son of the 2nd Marquess of Anglesey. As a younger son, Lord Alexander Paget, who was to become father of the 6th Marquess and grandfather of the present Marquess, had to be somewhat parsimonious and used to send his valet by 2nd class rail and his wife and children by 3rd class while he travelled 1st class. The Earl of Uxbridge was the eldest son of the 2nd Marquess and succeeded his father in 1869, so this picture would be taken during the 1860s. He was briefly the Liberal M.P. for South Staffordshire, in which constituency was the majority of the family acres and the ancestral home of the Pagets at Beaudesert Hall, built in the late sixteenth century and demolished 1930–35.

By courtesy of the Marquess of Anglesey

Alice Anne, the daughter of Sir Graham Graham-Montgomery and 3rd and last Duchess of Buckingham, sitting beneath a Grecian frieze by the south portico of Stowe House c.1890. After the death of the Duke, she was to marry the 1st Earl Egerton of Tatton Park who was chairman of the Manchester Ship Canal. Her first husband had also had industrial and financial interests, although in his case, by force of circumstances. The 2nd Duke of Buckingham had bankrupted himself within eight years of his succession by purchasing estates on borrowed money and by excessive personal expenditure. He had evidently inherited the intemperate character of his father, who had actually taken cannon from his yacht ashore in 1830 with a view to physically combating electoral reform. Portrayed in Disraeli's *Coningsby* as the Duke of Agincourt, the 2nd Duke was compelled to sell many of his estates – amongst them, Aston Clinton to Sir Anthony de Rothschild and Itchen Abbas to the banker Alexander Baring, Lord Ashburton – and the entire contents of Stowe. The sale took 40 days, from August to October 1848, realising £75,562. The prospect of a negligible inheritance compelled the 3rd Duke to take what was, until the 1880s at least, the exceptional step for an aristocrat of entering the world of commerce in an executive position. He became chairman of the London & North Western Railway from 1852–61 and one of the Lords of the Treasury, besides representing Buckingham in the Commons for 11 years. In 1875 he left England to become Governor of Madras until 1880, five years before his marriage to Alice Anne.

Michael Brand/National Monuments Record

Our view of Victorian mores has probably been unfairly influenced by the photographic legacy, which usually depicts unsmiling figures in a stiff formal pose. Their expressions rarely indicate a sense of fun, and pictures of such antics are still more scarce. The length of exposure necessary during the Victorian era meant that pictures had to be posed, and the care behind this composition of skaters on the frozen lake at Eastwell Park in Kent suggests that the gentleman on his back intended to be a cause of amusement. Harsher winters than we currently enjoy made skating a much more fashionable pastime, doubtless helped by the presence of a lake in the grounds of many a country house. Eastwell Park was for centuries the home of the earls of Winchelsea & Nottingham, reaching its final form under the guidance of the architect Joseph Bonomi. After a training in Rome, Bonomi came to England at the invitation of Robert Adam. Bonomi also designed Longford Hall in Shropshire, Great Packington Church in Warwickshire, and the mausoleum at Blickling. All that remains at Eastwell is the neo-Jacobean gatehouse, the house being demolished in 1926. The collection of notable monuments in the grounds went to the Victoria & Albert Museum in 1968.

By courtesy of the Earl of Cawdor

Rt Hon. Sir John Eldon Gorst (1835–1916) at The Grange, Erdington, Birmingham, home of Sir Benjamin Stone, in 1905. Born in Preston, Sir John went into the civil service, becoming Civil Commissioner of Waikato, New Zealand. He was then called to the Bar, becoming a Q.C. and Solicitor General in 1885. Later a Financial Secretary to the Treasury, he also represented Cambridge, Chatham and Cambridge University as a Conservative in the Commons. He changed his allegiance and unsuccessfully contested his birthplace for the Liberals. Lady Randolph Churchill recalled that 'his stern countenance belied him, and he could make himself very pleasant. . . . Sir John had a music-loving soul, and many were the occasions when he and I and Arthur Balfour went off to the ''Monday Pops'', to listen to the sweet strains of Joachim and Norman Neruda.'

Sir Benjamin Stone Collection, Birmingham Library

Broke Turnor   Captain Bastard   Henry Yorke R.N.

Sir John Thorold   Montagu Thorold   John Thorold   Hon. Henry Cole

Neither the whereabouts of this haystack nor the reason for the picnic are known, although several of the gentlemen lived in Lincolnshire. It can be established that the photograph was taken before 1866, for in that year Sir John Thorold, 11th Baronet, whose seat was Syston Old Hall, died. He was married to a daughter of Col Hildyard of Flintham Hall, and his younger son, Montagu Thorold, was son-in-law to Captain Bastard. John Thorold was to succeed his father as 12th Baronet and became M.P. for his home town of Grantham. Henry Yorke was knighted in 1902 for services to the Admiralty, and married the daughter of the Earl of Wemyss in 1882. The Turnors were a well-known Lincolnshire family, owning Little Ponton Hall near Grantham and Little Panton Hall near Wragby. The Hon. Henry Cole was the son of the Earl of Enniskillen and M.P. for the town before accepting the Chiltern Hundreds.

By courtesy of the Earl of Cawdor

Frivolity at St Leonard's Hill, Clewer, near Windsor, in June 1891. The Princess of Wales is tying the handkerchief, the gentleman on the left is the Duke of Clarence & Avondale, and to his right is the Hon. Julie Stonor. Princess Maud of Wales is in the centre, without a hat, and behind is the Hon. Oliver Montagu. The Duke of Clarence became engaged to Princess May of Teck 18 months after this picture was taken and died shortly afterwards. The Hon. Julie Stonor, with whom Edward, Prince of Wales was 'more or less in love' (according to Lady Geraldine Somerset), was the daughter of Lord Camoys of Stonor Park, near Henley-on-Thames, which has recently been opened to the public. Prince George had shown affection for Miss Stonor during her frequent visits to Sandringham, following the early death of her mother in 1883, but in 1891 she married the Marquis d'Hautpoul. Princess Maud of Wales (1869–1938) was the third daughter of Edward VII and was born at Buckingham Palace. In 1896 she married Prince Charles of Denmark who became King Haakon VII nine years later. St Leonard's was formerly known as Gloucester Lodge and was built by Thomas Sandby (1721–98) for the Countess of Waldegrave, afterwards Duchess of Gloucester. In 1872 it was bought by Sir Francis Tress Barry who had the house virtually rebuilt by C.H. Howell, three of Sandby's major rooms being left untouched. Sir Francis had been engaged in commerce at Bilbao where he was also vice-consul. After settling at St Leonard's Hill, he was appointed consul-general of the Republic of Ecuador in the United Kingdom.

Reproduced by gracious permission of Her Majesty The Queen

Left: A.A. Milne and Roland Kitson jumping an impromptu hurdle of walking sticks in the grounds of Gledhow Hall near Leeds. The occasion is not known. Born in 1882, A.A. Milne graduated from Cambridge and eked out a meagre living as a journalist until offered the assistant editorship of *Punch* in 1906. After fighting on the Western Front, he returned to work as a full-time writer. He suffered from the legacy of creating Pooh Bear, making the task of establishing a reputation for his serious plays and novels the more difficult.

Leeds Archives

The gentlemen of the Bootle-Wilbrahams family paying homage to the fair sex on the steps of Lathom House, near Ormskirk in Lancashire in 1904. The early eighteenth-century house was then the home of the 2nd Earl of Lathom, who was a major in the Horse Guards. His mother had been killed in a carriage accident near Lathom House in 1897, and his father, the 1st Earl, had been Lord Chamberlain of the royal household and Captain of the Yeomen of the Guard. The earldom became extinct in 1930, five years after Lathom House had been largely razed.

By courtesy of Lord Skelmersdale

Previous page: A group taken at Luton Hoo on 8 November 1886. From left to right: —, M. de Falbe, Miss Hawkes (seated), Ida Falbe (in Sedan chair), Hugh Fraser (on floor), Duchess of Teck, Prince Adolphus of Teck (standing by chair), Count Koziebrodski (on floor behind small table), —, Mme de Falbe with Willy, Princess Victoria Mary of Teck, —, ? Mme de Florian.

Luton Museum

Below: The scene at Belsay Castle in August 1905 when the tenants, workmen and servants of the Belsay and Allenford estates were entertained in the castle grounds in honour of the wedding of Sir Arthur E. Middleton's son Hugh to Mary Katherine, elder daughter of Rear Admiral Samuel Long. Hugh Middleton (1879–1914) had been a lieutenant in the Navy and then a commander in the R.N.V.R. Sir Arthur Middleton (1838–1933) had held the usual aristocratic or gentry position of High Sheriff and had been M.P. for Durham. About 130 people sat down to luncheon. After the loyal toast had been honoured, the health of the bride and groom was proposed. The *Newcastle Daily Journal* reported that 'Mr Leiper of Bygate proposed the health of Sir Arthur Middleton, and spoke of the good feeling which existed between Sir Arthur and his tenantry, a remark which was received with loud applause.' Sir Arthur responded and at about 3.00 pm the party was joined by the wives and families and 'other residents' on the estates:

> A programme of sports for the children and young people had been organised, which excited much interest, and dancing was also indulged in during the afternoon, and afterwards, in the tent, from 7 to 10, a Punch and Judy show and conjuring exhibition . . . was very much appreciated. About 4.30 pm over 400 sat down to tea. The music, supplied by the Ashington Orchestral Society, was all that could be desired. . . . The numerous prizes for the various sports during the afternoon were given by Sir Arthur and the Misses Middleton. . . . The playing of 'God Save the King' by the band brought to a close a red letter day at Belsay.

By courtesy of Sir Stephen Middleton

Right: The engagement photograph of the Duke of Clarence and Avondale, eldest son of Edward, Prince of Wales, and Princess Mary of Teck, daughter of the Duke of Teck, who became engaged in December 1891 while staying at Luton Hoo where this photograph was taken. Tragically, the Duke of Clarence shortly after caught influenza and pneumonia and died at Sandringham in January 1892, ending his younger brother's hope of a lifetime in the Royal Navy.

In the following year, Princess Mary married his brother George, Duke of York, to become Queen Mary in 1910, and it was a sad irony that he too was to die at Sandringham of influenza. Her childhood was over-shadowed by the indebtedness of her parents. The Duke and Duchess of Teck were spending twice their income and tradesmen were threatening them with the indignity of an execution in an attempt to recover the £18,000 they were owed. The economies which Princess Mary practised, such as making her own dresses, were to remain a lifelong concern.

She was the only Queen to be crowned Empress of India in person when she attended the great durbar in Delhi in December 1911. Queen Victoria described her as an 'excellent, useful-and good wife'. She was very active with good works on the state at Sandringham, calling on the Rector to ask him for a list of the sick and old pensioners as soon as she arrived in Norfolk. She would then visit them, taking a useful gift such as a bed-jacket or beverages.

Luton Museum

The Buchanan-Riddells being pulled by their tenantry in the grounds of their home at Hepple after their wedding.

Northumberland County Record Office

Above right: As a mark of respect and often gratitude, it was customary for estate workers and tenants to greet a landowner or his offspring when returning from a special occasion. Here the tenants and estate workers around Tarland escort the eldest son of the Earl of Aberdeen, Lord Haddo, and his bride to their home at Cromar House. The marriage had been solemnised at the Scottish Presbyterian Church in London on 6 August 1906. From there, the couple and Lord and Lady Aberdeen were conveyed by electric brougham to Lord Aberdeen's town house in Grosvenor Street for the reception, and thence by train to Aboyne for their honeymoon at Cromar House. The village of Tarland was decorated with flags and an arch composed of ivy, the Gordon crest, heather and wild flowers, and bearing the word 'Welcome' had been built across the road at the bridge over Tarland Burn. The schoolchildren had been given a holiday at the request of Lord Aberdeen, and shortly before midday they had marched to Cromar House with two pipers at their head. Lord Haddo's carriage was drawn up the drive by the tenants to the house, where cake and wine were served, followed by the inevitable speeches.

By courtesy of the Marchioness of Aberdeen

Centre right: The army was a natural career for many of the younger sons of the aristocracy and gentry. There were roughly 3,000 commissions in the army in the first half of the nineteenth century and they were reserved for 'the connections of this class of society'. Money was vital to purchase promotion, one's uniform and equipage for campaigns and it was not uncommon during the Napoleonic wars for eager would-be officers and aides-de-camp to resort to gambling to acquire sufficient

means. So, quite apart from the natural identification and concern of a ruling élite with the means of enforcing its power, landowners were generally willing to allow volunteer regular regiments the use of their estates at certain times. Here the Royal Buckinghamshire Hussars are encamped in the grounds of Stowe in 1910, with the south front in the background. By the time Capability Brown started as an under-gardener at Stowe in 1740 at the age of 25, Charles Bridgeman, William Kent and Vanbrugh had all helped to create grounds which prompted Lord Percival to write in 1724 that Stowe had 'gained the reputation of being the finest seat in England'. The mansion itself was splendid enough, although later further improved by Robert Adam, but it was the number of temples and monuments scattered throughout the grounds that made Stowe unique.

G. Clarke

Below right: During a particularly enjoyable three-week visit to Blair Castle by Queen Victoria and Prince Albert during 1844, the privilege of forming a private army was, perhaps mischievously, conferred upon the 7th Duke of Atholl and his heirs. The Atholl Highlanders are seen here on parade in front of the castle in 1883. It is a unique right, and the army is currently 80 strong and meets on parade twice a year. The 7th Duke was typical of many Highland landowners in his energetic concern for the region during the Victorian era. He served on the board of that aristocratic institution, the Highland Railway, and an engine was named after him. The 8th Duke fought in the Sudan and, after the Battle of Omdurman had ended the short-lived empire of the self-proclaimed Mahdi, brought back the pinnacle of the Mahdi's tomb which he had placed on the tower in the right of the picture. Blair was probably the last castle in the British Isles to be beseiged, in 1745.

By courtesy of the Duke of Atholl

Presentation of colours to the 5th, 6th and 7th Battalions of the Cheshire Regiment by King Edward VII at Eaton Hall on 17 December 1909. The grounds of the country houses were frequently chosen for such occasions for the very good reason that major landowners were often the nominal heads of their county regiment. The prominence of the clergy is noteworthy. Eaton Hall was and still is the home of the dukes of Westminster, although Alfred Waterhouse's splendid recreation of the already much-altered seventeenth-century hall was demolished in 1961. Waterhouse spent £600,000 transforming the house into what Pevsner regarded as the most ambitious exercise in Gothic Revival domestic architecture in the country. The Cheshire Regiment was one of the few regiments which did not experience amalgamation under the Cardwell reforms of 1881. The base of the 1st Batallion was Londonderry and that of the 2nd was Jubbolpore, Central Provinces. The 3rd Battalion was titled the Royal Cheshire Militia and the territorial force was made up of the 4th, 5th, 6th and 7th Battalions. Even in the dismal weather, the parade must have been a colourful spectacle – the Cheshires' uniform was a scarlet tunic with buff facings and a blue forage cap.

Radio Times Hulton Picture Library

Above right: The Buckingham and Winslow Volunteers at Claydon House in 1861; the rifle regiment was formed in 1860 under a misapprehension that Napoleon III was about to invade. In 1863, the five local Rifle Volunteer companies were amalgamated to form a battalion which was later to take part in the Boer War. Claydon's owner Sir Harry Verney, was a model landlord, draining and reclaiming land, building cottages and schools, planting trees and taking an active role in poor-law work. He knew George Stephenson, and studied and welcomed railways which impinged on his estate. For 52 years he represented Buckingham in the Commons as a Liberal, supporting reformist legislation such as factory acts and the abolition of army purchase and slavery. The experience of cholera epidemics in Aylesbury and Paris led Sir Harry to become instrumental in the establishment of a county hospital in the former town. This concern made natural the support he was to give to his famous sister-in-law. The lady of Claydon House, when this view was taken, was Frances Parthenope, Lady Verney, née Nightingale, elder sister of Florence. Frances Parthenope had married Sir Harry in 1858 and became absorbed with the history of the Verney family, editing the extraordinary collection of Verney letters and papers which affords us rare insight into the life of a landed family in the seventeenth century. In the mid-eighteenth century, Claydon was enlarged to rival Stowe by Ralph, the sad and improvident 2nd Earl Verney. His grandiose plans bankrupted him and his successor was obliged to demolish most of his additions, leaving only the west wing, which contains perhaps the most exuberant wood carving in the country.

By courtesy of Sir Ralph Verney

Right: Gladstone and the 7th Earl of Aberdeen (with chin on hand) on the steps of Haddo House. It was under the 7th Earl's grandfather, the 4th Earl when Prime Minister between 1852–5, that Gladstone began his career as one of Britain's finest chancellors. He was a regular visitor to Haddo during the 4th Earl's lifetime. John Campbell, the 7th Earl, became Viceroy of Ireland in 1886 and Governor-General of Canada from 1893–8. After his retirement, he and his wife installed their eldest son, the Earl of Haddo, in Haddo House and went to live in the House of Cromar at Tarland.

By courtesy of the Marchioness of Aberdeen

Mrs Goschen   Lady Carew   Lord Carew   Duchess of   Lady Knutsford
Rutland

Lord Eustace   Duc d'Aumale   Lady Cadogan   Lady Londonderry   Duchess of
Cecil   Manchester

Lord Lothian   Lord Halsbury   M. Waddington (French   Mme Waddington
Ambassador)

Rustem Pasha (Turkish   Sir Henry
Ambassador)   Drummond Wolfe

Senor J.L. Albareda   M. de Stael (Russian   Count Hatzfeldt (German   (Persian)   Sir Henry
(Spanish Ambassador)   Ambassador)   Ambassador)   Rawlinson

Lady Salisbury   Lord Salisbury   (Persian)

Prince of Wales   Shah of Persia   Princess of   (Persian)
Wales

Left: In July 1889, a garden party for the Shah of Persia was given by the Prime Minister, Lord Salisbury, at his home, Hatfield House. It was the 3rd Marquess (1830–1903) who restored the Cecil family to the position of national importance it had enjoyed in Elizabethan times under William Cecil, Lord Burghley. Queen Victoria described him as 'my greatest Prime Minister', and Lord Curzon referred to him as 'that strange, powerful, inscrutable and brilliant obstructive deadweight at the top'. An intellectual and deeply religious man, he was a Fellow of All Souls' College and Chancellor of the University of Oxford. He was also interested in science and was one of the first to install electricity and a telephone in his home. The electric light system was rigged up in 1881, only a year after Sir William Armstrong's home at Cragside was equipped with electric light by Joseph Swan, inventor of the incandescent light; but the system proved unsafe, the wires on the long gallery ceiling occasionally bursting into flame, compelling the family to hurl cushions at the fire to put it out. Lady Salisbury impressed Lady Randolph Churchill as a woman of great strength of character: 'One could not help liking her, notwithstanding her rather brusque manner. I fancy she detested affectations of any kind, and her masterly mind must have disdained the ordinary society twaddle to which she was often called upon to listen.' Sir Henry Rawlinson (1810–95) was a noted orientalist and his intimate knowledge of central Asian affairs gave him great influence over Salisbury's policies. Lord Halsbury was Lord Chancellor, and, ironically, Lord Lothian had been on Sir James Outram's staff in Persia during the war over Herat in 1856–7. Lord Lothian's principal homes were Newbattle Abbey, near Dalkeith, and Blickling Hall in Norfolk, which was given to the National Trust by his descendants in 1940. The Shah, Nasr ed-Din, had been disposed towards constitutional progress until the failure of constitutional government in Turkey in 1876. Thereafter he preferred 'ministers who do not know

whether Brussels is a city or a cabbage'. Lady Randolph Churchill wrote that his

> vagaries kept society amused and interested. A real barbarian, it was with difficulty that he was induced to conform to western habits. Many were the stories circulated about him. One night, at a banquet at Buckingham Palace, he was asked to give his arm to the late Queen Victoria. He refused, having made up his mind to take in a lady whose voluminous proportions had attracted his attention. Much pressure had to be brought to bear before he was prevailed upon to change his mind. With reluctance and a cross face, he dragged the Queen along as he strode into the dining-room. He thought the Duke of Sutherland too wealthy a subject and advised Edward, Prince of Wales, to have his head off when he reached the throne.

Nasr ed-Din was assassinated in 1896.

Reproduced by gracious permission of
Her Majesty The Queen

Above: A political garden party in the grounds of Wombwell Hall, near Gravesend in Kent, on 31 August 1898. The party was given by Mr J.H. Dudley Ryder M.P. and the Hon. Mrs Ryder to acknowledge the work of the local party members in the recent by-election. Nearly 500 invitations were issued, including all councillors and members of School Boards, irrespective of their politics. The *Gravesend and Dartford Reporter* described the proceedings, which lasted from 3.30 to 6.30 pm. Refreshments were served and

> selections of music were discoursed by the String Band 1st K.V.A. and the Northfleet Temperance Silver Prize Band . . . . Juggling by a Chinese conjuror and other entertainment was also included in the programme, and the weather being all that could be desired, that which was unique in the political annals of the borough passed off with every satisfaction.

Wombwell Hall was erected *c*.1860 by Thomas Colyer on the site of an earlier hall and was leased from Thomas Colyer-Ferguson by Mr Dudley-Ryder for three months in 1898. Mr Dudley-Ryder later became the 5th Earl of Harrowby.

By courtesy of the Earl of Harrowby

Above & below left: Sir John Benjamin Stone (1838–1914) was a Birmingham manufacturer who became such a successful amateur photographer that he was appointed official photographer for the coronation of George V in 1911. He travelled widely, visiting Japan, China, the West Indies, Asia Minor, the Rocky Mountains and the Amazon basin, writing and publishing his experiences on his return. He was Conservative M.P. for East Birmingham from 1895 to 1909 at a time when Joseph Chamberlain held West Birmingham. His home at The Grange, Erdington, was then in a semi-rural environment and was the venue of garden parties given for political purposes. This one was given on 29 July 1901 in appreciation of the effort made by constituency workers in the election. Such occasions may be said to have gradually replaced the contributions to charitable work made by landed society, partly out of a sense of *noblesse oblige* and partly to maintain support for the landowner's candidate. With the enfranchisement of the middle and lower classes, charitable contributions on the larger estates fell from around 4–7% of gross income to 1–2%. This was also attributable to the gradual takeover by local government of charitable organisations which had once looked to the local landowner for their main support, such as schools, hospitals and friendly societies.

Sir Benjamin Stone Collection, Birmingham Library

The visit of the Rt Hon. and Mrs Joseph Chamberlain (1836–1914) to Sandon Hall, Staffordshire, in July 1906. It was the occasion of a weekend party to which the distinguished guests travelled by train from Euston, a special stop being made at Sandon. The landau which conveyed Chamberlain to the hall stopped for an inspection of the new Workmen's Institute in the village, where the horses were unharnessed and members of the cricket team drew the landau by ropes up the drive leading to the hall. Half-way up they were relieved by estate workmen. School children were outside the hall cheering as he arrived and the crowd encouraged the ex-Colonial Secretary to make an impromtu speech. Chamberlain's home was Moor Green Hall in Birmingham where he had been in manufacturing until entering politics. From 1876 until his death in 1914 he sat in the Commons for Birmingham West, succeeding the 3rd Earl of Harrowby as President of the Board of Trade in 1880. The host, the 5th Earl of Harrowby (whose 21st birthday celebrations are shown in the photograph on **page 74**) is wearing the double-breasted suit and standing to the right of Joseph Chamberlain, in the lighter coloured suit. Chamberlain's wife, his third, was Mary Endicott, daughter of a United States supreme court judge, and is seated just in front of him. Sandon Hall was built in Jacobean style in 1852 to the designs of William Burn, replacing the structure burnt down in 1848.

By courtesy of the Earl of Harrowby

A school feast in August 1869 at Garnons, Mansell Gamage, Herefordshire, home of the Cotterell family. Landowners frequently supported the Anglican National Schools in villages on or near their estates, and were spurred into more vigorous action by the threat of democratically controlled Board Schools created by the Education Act of 1870. The improving quality of Board Schools made survival difficult for voluntary schools and this function of the local squire had all but ended by World War I. The grounds at Garnons were landscaped by Humphry Repton in 1791, a red book being produced, in which Repton expressed his ideas.

> The character of a place will take its distinguishing marks from the united consideration of its situation and the extent of territory surrounding. Both these at Garnons require a degree of greatness which neither the house nor Grounds at present indicate. It is not necessary to build a palace to produce the character of Greatness, but a house which is the seat of Hospitality, and where according to the custom of Herefordsnire, not only the neighbouring Families but even their servants and horses may receive a welcome, must necessarily form such a mass of building as will give an air of Greatness to the general appearance. I am particularly happy in this instance that I act in concert with such acknowledged powers as those of James Wyatt Esq . . .

Wyatt's proposal for a castellated mansion did not materialise. Garnons was mostly demolished in 1957.

National Monuments Record

Above right: A treat at Haddo House on 12 August 1893 for the children living on the estate of the Earl of Aberdeen. The party was held to mark the appointment of the Earl as Governor-General of Canada, which position he held for five years. The 7th Earl had succeeded to the title in extraordinary and distressing circumstances: his brother, the 6th Earl, had lived a life of adventure on the sea, believing 'there is no better or happier place in the world than a good small *American* vessel: a person has few or no temptations to contend with', but in 1870 he was swept overboard in a gale. It took several years to establish the manner of his death, before the 7th Earl could succeed to the title. An academic and holder of numerous degrees, the 7th Earl was Viceroy of Ireland before his Canadian appointment and was created Marquess of Aberdeen and Temair in 1916.

By courtesy of the Marchioness of Aberdeen

Right: The 21st birthday of the heir to the title or estate was the most important family occasion. Events such as birth, the attainment of majority, marriage and death were generally marked by celebrations or mourning which involved the local community and served to emphasise and enhance the standing of the family. It is difficult now to imagine the atmosphere with which such occasions were invested. Only Royal pageants retain a vestige of this aura with its element of paying homage to an ancient and worthy lineage. This was the scene at Acton Reynold in Shropshire when Sir Roland James Corbet, son of the late Sir Walter Orlando Corbet, reached his majority in 1913. Sir Walter, who had died three years before, was Deputy Lieutenant and High Sheriff of the county, and served as a captain in the Coldstream Guards, participating in the Egyptian Expedition in 1882. His son served from the beginning of World War I and was killed in 1915. Acton Reynold is a large Victorian mansion, seven miles south of Shrewsbury, incorporating a considerable part of the Corbets' seventeenth-century home.

The Publisher

On Saturday 22 August 1885, the presumptive heir to the Earldom of Harrowby, J.H. Dudley-Ryder, was given a garden party to mark his coming-of-age. His father, the 3rd Earl of Harrowby's brother, was a partner in Coutts Bank and the family lived at High Ashurst near Dorking. The garden party was accompanied by the Band of the Grenadier Guards and attended by social equals of the family. On the Monday, a party was given for the people of Headley and tradesmen, while the estate workers were entertained on the Tuesday. The *Surrey Standard* reported that the party on Monday went 'a long way to disprove the Radical view that the English aristocracy is unpopular with the people. Perhaps nothing could be advanced wider of the mark . . . .' The paper detailed the charitable work done by the family and concluded that

> respect for the English aristocracy is deep seated in the hearts of the people of the country and, on the other hand, our noble families are ever ready and anxious to promote the enjoyment and happiness of those around them. It is well that this feeling mutually exists, and no doubt proceedings like those of Saturday and Monday last go far to cement and strengthen it.

By courtesy of the Earl of Harrowby

A lunch given to the tenants and local friends of Lord and Lady Armstrong at Cragside on Saturday 11 October 1913 to commemorate the 21st birthday of their son and heir, the Hon. William Watson-Armstrong. The *North Mail* reported the occasion:

> A charming little incident in the gathering, reminiscent of old world custom, was the drinking of the heir's health from the magnificent loving cup, the present from Lord and Lady Armstrong which was passed round the table for each guest to drink from. Other toasts, including success to Rothsbury and agriculture, were proposed, the latter by Sir John Buchanan-Riddell of Hepple and the former by Col Adye.

The festivities lasted several days and included a ball for employees and the townspeople on the Friday night and a garden party before the Armstrongs moved to their other seat at Bambrugh Castle for a further round of celebration. Bunting floated from every house in Rothbury, the church bells were rung and commemorative mugs were given fo the schoolchildren.

Cragside was extended from a small lodge to the house seen today by Norman Shaw between 1869 and 1884 for the 1st Lord Armstrong, accompanied by the creation of a landscape and park that entailed the planting of seven million trees. The house was the first in the country to be lit with electricity and the use of hydraulics for various functions reflected Lord Armstrong's specialisation in that field which, together with armaments, had made his fortune. The dining room at Cragside was inadequate for a party of this size so it was held in the drawing room, which was built in 1883–4. Behind the photographer is the huge chimney-piece – 20 feet of carved alabaster over an inglenook lined with marble. Some of the pictures in the room are now hanging at Bambrugh Castle.

By courtesy of Jeremy M. Blake

Below: The Victorian era saw greater attention paid to the development of scientific farming and more efficient agricultural methods than any previous age. Economic historians date the agricultural revolution rather earlier, but the effect and benefit of inventions naturally take time to be felt. Mutual improvement meetings of farmers were made famous by the Holkham gatherings arranged at his Norfolk estate by Thomas Coke (1752–1842) who became 1st Earl of Leicester. This is a dairy conference at Broughton Castle, Westmorland, in 1892. Pevsner refers to it as Broughton Tower and describes it as a spacious mansion built around a fourteenth-century pele tower by the Gilpin Sawrey family in the mid-eighteenth century.

Above right: Fire has always been the main fear of country-house owners. Until this century and the adaptation of the internal combustion engine to fire-fighting equipment, even professional services were relatively crude, relying on Merryweather steam engines for pumping which were drawn by horses to the fire. Nor did the usual distance between a remote country house and the nearest fire service help matters. It is little wonder that some owners purchased their own fire engines and the 3rd Duke of Sutherland, with his love of mechanical matters, played a prominent role in developing fire-fighting services generally. The loss of art treasures and fine libraries in country-house fires over the years has been appalling. The experience of such a catastrophe was vividly described by Galsworthy in *A Modern Comedy*, when Soames's feverish determination saved most of his art collection from a fire at Mapledurham. This is the scene at Brampton Park near Huntingdon the day after a fire in 1907. Some of the remains were incorporated into a smaller house with interiors which Pevsner described as sumptuous. The house was built in Elizabethan times on the site of a house said to be ruinous by 1328, rebuilt in the mid-seventeenth century and again by Lady Olivia Sparrow in about 1820. Lady Olivia, a philanthropist and friend of Wilberforce and Hannah More, lived there until her death in 1863. The property descended to her daughter's great grandson, the Duke of Manchester, and in 1889 it became an institution for the care of stammerers.

Below right: Firemen at Stourhead in Wiltshire after a fire on 16 April 1902 had gutted the central part of the house. The picture gallery in one wing and the library in the other were happily unharmed. Sir Henry Hoare then commissioned Sir Aston Webb, architect of the Admiralty Arch and Britannia Royal Naval College, and Doran Webb of Salisbury, to restore the buildings largely to their original form, although the roof over the hall was raised and ornamentation altered or added. Designed by Colen Campbell, the house was one of the first in the country built in the style derived from the villas built by Palladio for Venetian noblemen around Vicenza. The villa built in Chiswick for one of the keenest propagators of Palladio's ideas, the Earl of Burlington, was not even begun until 1725, whereas Stourhead was largely complete in 1724.

Left: The Victorians enjoyed dressing up and welcomed the opportunity to create outlandish costumes. The days when some exertion in the creation of entertainment would be regarded as a chore were still distant. The play to be performed in 1904, in the two photographs, by the de Harnel family and maid servants of Middleton Hall in Warwickshire is not known – perhaps they were ambitious enough to tackle *The Mikado*. Amateur theatricals in country houses go back to the sixteenth century, when strolling minstrels and players would travel from house to house to entertain the lord and his retinue. Some of the wealthier aristocrats, such as the Earl of Leicester, had their own troupe of players who were often at liberty to visit other houses when not required by their lord. The best-known visual representation of medieval theatricals is the strange painting in the National Portrait Gallery of Sir Henry Unton, depicting masqued performers accompanied by six musicians. For the next two centuries plays seem to have passed out of favour as suitable entertainment in the country house, perhaps due to the growing popularity of musical evenings, balls and dinner parties on the one hand, and the influence of puritanism on the other. Yet professional theatre during the Restoration period prospered, although the plays were strongly satirical and often aimed at the very people best able to afford private performances. A renaissance of amateur theatricals began in the 1770s and continued into Victorian times, occasioning the construction of special theatres at some houses, such as Chatsworth, Wynnstay in Denbighshire, and Wargrave in Berkshire. Fanny Price in Jane Austen's *Mansfield Park* (1814) still regards the idea of performing a romantic play as rather improper, and the readiness with which the characters in the novel subscribe to its performance is intended as an index to their moral values.

Sir Benjamin Stone Collection, Birmingham Library

Above: A group of rather sombre-looking servants at York Cottage, dressed for a Fancy Dress Ball in January 1905. York Cottage was formerly known as Bachelor's Cottage and built as an annexe for male guests at Sandringham until Edward VII gave it to the Duke of York as a wedding present. Even as George V, he and Queen Mary continued to live there until the death of his mother in 1925 while they were visiting the estate, so attached was he to its domesticity. The Duchess of York was less enamoured with what most regarded as an undesirable and unworthy residence for a king. Harold Nicolson remarked that 'the rooms inside . . . are indistinguishable from those of any Surbiton or Upper Norwood home'. Balls were the most elaborate and formal entertainment offered by country-house life. Turnpike roads had enabled large gatherings to be held outside London and, by the 1780s, 400 guests were being invited to balls at Hatfield House. Fires would be lit along the drive and near the house to guide the carriages and enable footmen and drivers to keep warm. Masked and fancy dress balls were popular in the nineteenth century, the former providing an element of mystery that did away with the usual formality of dance cards.

Reproduced by gracious permission of Her Majesty the Queen

Left: The idea of the rather effeminate 5th Marquess of Anglesey (1875–1905) serving as a Lieutenant in the Royal Welsh Fusiliers seems incongruous, but it was his only occupation after leaving Eton, other than indulging his passion for jewellery and clothes. Within six years of succeeding to the title, he had accumulated debts of £544,000 despite receiving an annual income of £110,000. His jewellery was sold after his insolvency and realised £88,000. He converted the chapel at Plas Newydd into a theatre where he staged lavish productions, importing professional actors and actresses from London, generally to support him in the leading role. The chapel theatre was situated above the Rex Whistler room but was done away with in the 1930s to make room for two floors of bedrooms. The marriage of the 5th Marquess survived for only two years and he died without issue in Monte Carlo at the age of 30. The *Complete Peerage* came to the sad conclusion that 'he seems only to have existed for the purpose of giving a melancholy and unneeded illustration of the truth that a man with the finest prospects, may, by the wildest folly and extravagance, as Sir Thomas Browne says, "foully miscarry in the advantage of humanity, play away an uniterable life, and have lived in vain".'

The National Trust

Right: On 6 July 1912 was staged the Hinchingbrooke Historical Pageant in the grounds of the ancient Huntingdon house, portraying in the form of a precursor of *son et lumière*, the history of Hinchingbrooke.

The nuns were expelled from the Priory in 1535 and the estate given to Richard Cromwell. Queen Elizabeth visited the house in 1598, and five years later King James stayed on his way from the north to take possession of the English crown, having spent the previous night at Burleigh. At Hinchingbrooke, he

> had such entertainment as was not the like in any place before; there was such a plentie and varieties of meates and diversities of wines and the sellars open at every man's pleasure. Master Cromwell presented his Majestie with many rich and acceptable gifts, as a very great and fayre wrought standing coffer of gold, goodly horses, deep-mouthed hounds, divers hawkes of excellent wing, and at the remove gave fifty pounds amongst his Majestie's officers.

In the same year, master Oliver Cromwell, then attending the Grammar School at Huntingdon, met the future Charles I in the grounds of the home of his uncle (Sir Oliver) and tradition has it that the youths had not been long together before they quarrelled and came to blows. Lying just off the Great North Road, Hinchingbrooke became a favourite resting place with the King and this placed such a financial burden on Sir Oliver that he became bankrupt. He sold the estate to Sir Sidney Montagu, later 1st Earl of Sandwich, who was cousin and patron of Samuel Pepys. In the pageant, the 8th Earl took the part of the 1st Earl and was modestly named in the programme as Mr George Montagu.

Huntingdon Record Office

A garden party at Hinchingbrooke near Huntingdon in
1878. The house was then owned by the 7th Earl of
Sandwich (1811–84) who was Lord Lieutenant of the
county from 1841 until his death and colonel of the
county militia. Horace Walpole wrote to George Montagu
of Hinchingbrooke:

> Considering it is in Huntingdonshire, the situation is not so
> ugly nor melancholy as I expected, but I do not conceive
> what provoked so many of your ancestors to pitch their
> tents in that triste country, unless the Capulets loved fine
> prospects. The house of Hinchingbrooke is most comfortable,
> and just what I like; old, spacious, irregular, yet not vast or
> forlorn.

Garden parties became an increasingly popular form of
entertainment in the nineteenth century, often given for
specific rather than purely social reasons. The size of the
gathering, particularly in the case of political occasions,
was generally too large for the *hoi polloi* to be
accommodated in the house.

Huntingdon County Record Office

The house-party of Mr and Mrs Almeric Paget at Panshanger, Hertfordshire, on 18 July 1914. Panshanger had long been renowned for its house-parties, especially during the ownership of Lord Cowper, who entertained lavishly. Prime Ministers from Lord Melbourne, whose home at Brocket was nearby, to Balfour were regular guests. John Buchan frequently attended parties, later in the hope of meeting Susan Grosvenor whom he married in 1907. The political tone of the parties continued under Almeric Paget (1861–1949), who was M.P. for Cambridge from 1910–17 when he accepted the Chiltern Hundreds. The son of General Lord Alfred Paget, he married the daughter of the Hon. William Whitney, one time secretary of the United States Navy. He was created Baron Queenborough in 1918. Panshanger was purchased by the 5th Earl Cowper and drastically altered in 1808 by William Atkinson, a pupil of James Wyatt. The park was regarded as one of Repton's most perfect schemes, recorded in his Red Book. Queen Victoria visited the house in 1841 and towards the end of the century it became a venue for gatherings of society intellectuals, known as 'The Souls', which included George Curzon, Arthur Balfour, George Wyndham, and Herbert Asquith. The St. James's Gazette retrospectively described them as a circle of 'personages distinguished for their beauty, breeding, delicacy and discrimination of mind'. They met to discuss literature and the arts and to play charades; Emily Eden described the house as being 'full to the brim of vice, agreeableness, foreigners, and roués'. The shooting was commendable, and it was at Panshanger that Lord de Grey shot 52 birds out of 54 in one stand using only one hand. Done for a bet, he had two loaders and three guns. With the death of the Souls' patron, the 7th Earl Cowper, the earldom became extinct and on the death of his widow in 1913 the property was inherited by her niece and sold to the Pagets. Lady Desborough, who lived at Panshanger until her death in 1952, was the last occupant – her executors ordered demolition of the house.

Radio Times Hulton Picture Library

Left: Annie Cass, daughter of Sir John Cass of Bradford, married in 1887 Weetman Pearson, head of the engineering firm of S. Pearson & Son, who became Liberal M.P. for Colchester and was created Baron Cowdray in 1910. The association of Lord and Lady Cowdray with the north-east of Scotland began in 1907 when Lady Cowdray took a lease on Dunecht House near Aberdeen before purchasing the estate in 1912. In her concern to create employment she commissioned Sir Aston Webb to make extensive additions to the house and undertook improvements to the estate. It was the same motive which led to the selection of unemployed workmen in Stonehaven for the restoration of Dunnottar Castle, also owned by Lady Cowdray. She and her husband made many generous benefactions to the city and University of Aberdeen, such as the Cowdray Club for Girls and the Cowdray Hall beside the Art Gallery. Another of Lady Cowdray's causes was women's suffrage and a group of supporters are seen here at Dunecht during a garden party in September 1911. The Italianate house was of granite and begun in 1820, the earls of Crawford and Balcarres adding to the house during the century. The house was heated with hot water pipes, often concealed in ornamental cases with marble tops. Two gasometers supplied the house, stables, and home farm with gas for lighting, and a 'commodious cottage' had been erected for the 'Gas Manager'.

Radio Times Hulton Picture Library

Foxhunting was without doubt the most cohesive and unifying element in Victorian rural society. The excitement of the chase attracted people of every occupation in an atmosphere of unanimous bonhomie difficult to imagine with our contemporary experiences of hunt sabotage by opponents of blood sports. Until the eighteenth century, hunting had concentrated on the stag and hare rather than the fox, and ritual in the form of colourful attire and a code of conduct or etiquette was virtually absent. The first to breed hounds for hunting was Hugo Meynell of Quorndon Hall. From the 1800s, the number of hunts generally increased, and improved communications enabled more frequent escapes from the capital to participate in hunts. However, the construction of a railway could also pose an obstacle to the hunt, and it was common for engine drivers to be reminded by management that they should shut off steam and be prepared to allow the hunt to cross the line should they see one ahead. This group is gathered before Easton Neston in Northamptonshire in October 1887, with the Prince of Wales mounted on the horse second from left. The house was built *c*.1700 for Sir William Fermor by Nicholas Hawksmoor, who had worked closely with Wren and with Vanbrugh at Castle Howard. It was his first independent work.

Reproduced by gracious permission of
Her Majesty The Queen

Of the pursuits enjoyed by landed society, foxhunting was potentially the most expensive. With the development of organised foxhunting in the late eighteenth and early nineteenth centuries, the cost of maintaining a hunt was usually borne by subscription, but occasionally a landowner would foot the entire bill. The 5th Duke of Portland was spending £2,000 a year on hunting by the early 1800s. The kennels erected by the 3rd Duke of Richmond at Goodwood in 1787 cost £6,000, and now serve as the headquarters of Goodwood Golf Club. The Belvoir hounds consumed 34 tons of oatmeal in 1798, besides horseflesh, and the heating for the kennels required 48 tons of coal. The current argument of foxhunters that the sport is justified by being the most humane manner of eliminating a cruel predator is the antithesis of the Victorian outlook. It was then considered little short of an affront to rural society for foxes to be destroyed by any other method, simply because it reduced the number available for the hunt. An agent of the Duke of Cumberland wrote to an absentee landlord in 1858: 'There has been foul play with foxes . . . an unlooked for and shameful outrage that has taken place in foxhunting country . . . a tenant of yours has made it his business to destroy foxes on Anniscliffe Moor.' The Eglinton Foxhounds, seen here gathering at Cessnock Castle, Ayrshire, on 19 September 1911, sometimes used the railway to travel to or return from hunting country. Lord Eglinton had started the hunt in 1861, but gained a poor reputation from his gratuitous cruelty to his young huntsman, Tom Firr, who went to the Quorn. Firr has been described as the best huntsman in history. A day with Lord Eglinton's hounds during their first decade is described in *The Eustace Diamonds* by Trollope. The wife of the diamonds' late owner, Lizzie Greystock, is new to the sport and is surprised and dismayed at the expense: two hunters had cost £320. The crowd of Ayrshire hunting men was made up of 'a lord or two, a dozen lairds, two dozen farmers, and as many men of business out of Ayr, Kilmarnock, and away from Glasgow'. The day was rather a fiasco, two foxes being 'chopped', and a third ingloriously dug out in a drizzle. 'If this is hunting', said Lizzie, 'I really don't think so much about it.' 'It's Scotch hunting', replied Mrs Carbuncle.

Radio Times Hulton Picture Library

Right: The riding school at Welbeck Abbey, together with the tan gallop (*top*), was the second largest in the world, situated near the exit of the 5th Duke of Portland's $1\frac{1}{4}$-mile tunnel. The glass and iron-vaulted roof was built on cast-iron columns and was lit by 8,000 gas jets. The tan gallop provided a run of a quarter of a mile with no windows throughout its length. A tunnel led to the stables which held 94 horses when the 5th Duke died in 1879, and kept 45 grooms busy. In common with the maintenance of a pack of hounds, the upkeep of the stables could run away with huge sums: Lord Fitzwilliam's annual expenditure on his racing stables at Wentworth Woodhouse fluctuated between £1,500 and £3,000. Horses were kept for hunting, racing, the pulling of carriages, and occasionally for ploughing on the home farm, although at larger houses the farm buildings would generally be far removed from the domain. Duties in the stables entailed far more than grooming and feeding the horses. At Newby Hall in Yorkshire the tasks performed by stable hands in December 1892 included sturdy (hand) drilling, carting gravel, brush harrowing, making wardrobes, fetching coal from York for cottagers, rolling, working oak for the wardrobes, cleaning drains, picking stones in the park, lagging pipes in the hall, clearing roots, clearing cow dung, painting saddle room, repairing window shutters, whitewashing, painting greenhouses, repairing fences, spreading manure, and weighing beasts.

George Washington Wilson, King's College, Aberdeen

Left: Shooting was a popular sport long before
foxhunting. In common with the latter, shooting brought
the aristocracy and gentry together, both socially and
with a view to common policies of game preservation.
But conflicts arose between landlord and tenant farmer,
who blamed over-preservation of rabbits and hares for
the decimation of crops. Turnips and carrots were being
grown more widely with the new agricultural methods
and programmes of the early nineteenth century, and
these crops were particularly appealing to hares and
rabbits. Landowners generally responded by allowing
tenants to shoot running game, carrying out culls, or
even reimbursing farmers for damage. The concentration
of game in protected areas increased the temptation to
poach, producing in turn game laws with savage
penalties to try to protect the landowners' investment;
by the time of the accession of Queen Victoria, they
had been moderated somewhat but game preservation
continued to cause antagonism, not least amongst farmers
on the Sandringham estate as the Prince of Wales
worked to establish good reserves of game. The 3rd Earl
of Lichfield (1856–1918) is seen here shooting at Brocket
in December 1906. A Deputy Governor of the Hudson's
Bay Company, he was tragically killed, falling into the
river near his home at Shugborough while out duck
shooting alone one evening.

Reproduced by gracious permission of
Her Majesty The Queen

A royal shooting party at Heveningham Hall in Suffolk
on 22 November 1876. Standing are H.R.H. the Duke of
Cambridge and Colonel Bateson, while seated are Sir
Hugh Cholmeley, General Sir James MacDonald, Lord
Colville, and Lord Huntingfield; on the rugs are Colonel
the Hon. J.C. Vanneck and H.H. the Maharajah Duleep
Singh. H.R.H. The Duke of Cambridge was cousin to
Queen Victoria and chose to leave his native Hanover on

her accession. In command of the 17th Lancers, he
quelled a disturbance in Leeds in 1842 and became a
major general in 1845. During the Crimean War he was
present at Alma and Inkerman. Largely due to the
Queen's influence, he became commander-in-chief of the
British army in 1856, a post he held until 1895, during
which time he stubbornly resisted innovation. In his
private life he was less traditional, marrying an actress in
1847 in contravention of the Royal Marriage Act of 1772.
Sarah Fairbrother was a popular actress in burlesques
and pantomimes, and gave the Duke three sons before
leaving the stage in 1848, a year after their marriage.
H.R.H. The Duke of Cambridge was described in *Society
in London* as a 'bluff, fresh, hale country gentleman, with
something of the vigorous healthy frankness of the
English skipper, and something, too, of the Prussian
martinet; industrious, punctual, rising early, seeking rest
late, fond of life and its pleasures, of good dinners, good
cigars, pleasant women, of the opera, of the play.' Sir
Hugh Cholmeley lived at Easton Hall in Lincolnshire and
represented Grantham in the Commons from 1868–80.
General Sir James MacDonald was equerry and private
secretary to the Duke of Cambridge. Lord Colville, later
Baron Colville of Culross, Perthshire, was Gentleman of
the Bedchamber to the Prince Consort in the 1840s and
Chamberlain to the Prince of Wales from 1873–1901. He
followed the example of the Duke of Buckingham in
becoming chairman of a railway company, the Great
Northern, in 1880 but by the penultimate decade of the
century it was becoming an increasingly aristocratic
habit. Lord Huntingfield of Heveningham Hall was the
3rd Baron whose grandfather, Sir Gerrard Vanneck,
commissioned Sir Robert Taylor to build what became
the grandest Georgian mansion in Suffolk, with an
interior and orangery by Wyatt and grounds by
Capability Brown.

Suffolk Photographic Survey

A shooting party on 4 September 1877 at Elveden Hall in Suffolk, home of the Maharajah Duleep Singh, the portly gentleman seated to the right of the doorway. The Prince of Wales is seated to the left of the doorway, arm on hip. Duleep Singh was one of the most extraordinary figures amongst aristocratic circles in the third quarter of the nineteenth century. Born in 1838, the son of the Rajah of the Punjab, he held the title until the annexation of the Punjab by the East India Company at the end of the Sikh Wars of 1845–6. Although deposed, he was granted the enormous pension of £40,000 per annum which enabled him to live in great style when he made his home in England in 1854. He had become a Christian in the previous year. In 1863 he purchased Elveden Hall near Thetford and turned the Georgian house into an oriental extravaganza. The architect John Norton produced the designs that kept 350 men at work for three years. So much Carrara marble was imported that a railway had to be built to the house to carry it and other materials. The *battues* he gave there became famous and, together with the magnificence of his palace,

enhanced the reputation of the estate to such an extent that Duleep Singh was offered half a million pounds for it in 1878. He declined it. Two years later his extravagance necessitated an inquiry into his debts, leading to the sale of Elveden to Lord Iveagh for £150,000. Duleep Singh demanded that the government settle his debts and, when they refused, took passage for Bombay. He issued a political proclamation to the Sikhs calling on them to reclaim the Punjab, so the Viceroy of India had him stopped at Aden, where he abjured Christianity and re-embraced the Sikh faith. He then went to Russia, writing fiery letters about the perfidy of England. He ended his life in Paris, dying at the Hotel Tremouille in 1893. Lord Iveagh enlarged Elveden yet again, basing his designs on the Taj Mahal. To give some idea of the quality of shooting at Elveden, a party of six guns in five days of shooting in 1896 accounted for 4,961 pheasants, 1,081 partridges, 564 rabbits, 505 hares, and 3 woodcock.

Reproduced by gracious permission of
Her Majesty The Queen

Below: The game waggon at Studley Royal near Ripon in Yorkshire after a morning's shooting in November 1901. It was taken on one of the two day's shooting at the Marquess of Ripon's home which were described in an article in *Country Life*. The 24,000-acre estate was described as a veritable paradise for the sportsman and Lord de Grey, who shared with Lord Walsingham the reputation of being the finest shot in England, was quoted as saying that he had never seen birds fly higher or more strongly. One of the charms of shooting on the estate was attributed to the birds being genuinely wild, so that 'their flight when they are ready to be food for powder leaves nothing to be desired'. But this quality had naturally been achieved at the expense of quantity: up to and including 1897, a considerable number of pheasants was reared and the best weekly bag was 6,147 pheasants in 1896. Thereafter no more birds were reared and the best weekly bag in 1898 fell to 1,481. During the two days described, six guns accounted for 2,774 pheasants, 69 partridges, 89 hares, 144 rabbits and 1 woodcock. The design of game waggon was commended for preventing the crushing of the birds in a disorderly pile. It is interesting to note that the writer of the article felt it necessary to anticipate criticisms of cruelty, even in 1901 and to such an ostensibly sympathetic readership: 'It may be sad that so much brightness and beauty should perish in the twinkling of an eye; but emphatically the operation is not cruel, and it is certainly not easy.'

Museum of English Rural Life, University of Reading

Overleaf: All that is known about this photograph is that it was taken on 30 November 1886 by Frederick Thurston. It is reasonable to assume that it was taken somewhere in Bedfordshire as most of the Thurston family photographs were taken in their native county. The gathering would appear to be of local squires and farmers although the sophisticated game waggon suggests considerable affluence. It must have been a disappointing day for so many guns if the total bag is on display.

Luton Museum

Back row, left to right: Lord Gosford, Lady Emily Kingscote, Hon. Sidney Greville, Hon. George Curzon, Major-General Ellis, Lady Gosford, Rt. Hon. Arthur Balfour, Mrs W. Grenfell, Sir S. Scott, Lord Londonderry, Lady H. Stuart, Lady Lilian Spencer Churchill, Mr W. Grenfell, Prince Charles of Denmark, Lord Curzon.
Front row, left to right: Lord Chesterfield, Lady Randolph Spencer Churchill, Duchess of Marlborough, Princess of Wales, Rt. Hon. Henry Chaplin, Prince of Wales, Hon. Mrs George Curzon, Lady Londonderry, Princess Victoria of Wales, Princess Charles of Denmark.
On ground, left to right: Lady Sophie Scott, Duke of Marlborough, Lady Georgina Curzon.
A shooting party at Blenheim in November 1896.

Breakfast on such occasions was a ceremonious affair and no one would dream of beginning until all had assembled. Lunch in early Victorian times was a totally informal event, the shooters often eating something cold in the open and quickly returning to their sport. By 1896 lunch in the field had developed into an elaborate part of the house-party ritual. After occupying themselves with reading, writing or conversation during the morning, the ladies would walk or drive to the rendezvous where a large tent would have been erected. Portable stoves enabled hot food to be served, and at Sandringham the Prince of Wales would read out the morning's scores. The Prince enjoyed few things more than a grand *battue*, although he was not a particularly good shot nor over careful, on one occasion shooting a beater in the knee as he swung round for a hare. His gamekeepers were as smartly attired as any in Germany, wearing green velveteen coats and bowler hats with gold cords on shooting days. At the end of the day the bag would be laid out for inspection before being taken to the game larder.

The 4th Earl of Gosford was the Lord of the Bedchamber to the Prince of Wales from 1886–1901. George Curzon had achieved academic distinction at Balliol College, Oxford, and was Under Secretary of State for Foreign Affairs when this photograph was taken. He became Viceroy and Governor General of India two years later, and during his lifetime was successively created Baron, Earl and Marquess Curzon of Kedleston. Satirised by Max Beerbohm as 'Britannia's butler', he retired from politics, and in his retirement painstakingly restored the ruins of Bodiam and Tattershall castles, bequeathing them to the nation. Arthur Balfour was then First Lord of the Treasury and Leader of the House of Commons, becoming Prime Minister in 1902. Lady Lilian Spencer Churchill (1873–1951) was sister of the 9th Duke of Marlborough, seated on the ground. Viscount Curzon was the eldest son of the 3rd Earl Howe, succeeding to the title in 1900. The 10th Earl of Chesterfield had just retired as Treasurer of the Household. His principal residence was Holme Lacy in Herefordshire. Lady Londonderry was one of the most celebrated hostesses of her times. Lady Randolph Spencer Churchill was the widow of the 8th Duke of Marlborough's brother who

had died in the previous year. The 9th Duchess of Marlborough was Consuelo, daughter of the wealthy American industrialist William Vanderbilt. The Rt Hon. Henry Chaplin was M.P. for the Kesteven division of Lincolnshire and was created Viscount Chaplin in 1916. He had been married to the daughter of the 3rd Duke of Sutherland until her early death in 1881. Mary Curzon had married George Curzon in the previous year, and was the first and only American to hold such a responsibility in the greatest vice royalty in the world, for which *The Times* thought her well suited: 'By character, by personal charm, by a rare intelligence, Lady Curzon was admirably and perfectly fitted for this distinction.' Arthur Balfour was very fond of her, finding her 'intoxicating, delicious and clever'. She died aged only 36. Lady Georgina Curzon was the eleventh and last child of Lord Scarsdale, and sister to George Curzon.

Below right: The construction of railways in the highlands of Scotland transformed not only the shooting habits of the landed gentry but their seasonal movements too. It was not uncommon for the wealthier landowners in the Highlands to hire an entire train to convey their whole household – carriages, horses, dogs, *et alia* – from their English seat to Scottish home. The Duke of Sutherland moved on such a scale from Trentham to Dunrobin, and the Highland Railway, of which he was a Director, came to depend heavily on such custom. The attraction was the grouse moors, and the number of game keepers in Scotland almost doubled between 1836 and 1868. These are the hillmen and gamekeepers of the Atholl estate in 1886, taken at Blair Castle. Regular photographs were taken of them, reflecting the esteem in which they and their work were held.

Alex McDougall. Donald Rose.   Peter McDuff. Robert Stewart. Alex McAra. Wm Campbell.   W^m McAra.

Alex^r Gow.

James McDonald.   John Stewart. Ja^s Stewart. Donald McBeath. Robt Dow. Neil Irvine. Neil McBeath. Donald Stewart.

Deerstalking was one pursuit which obliged the would-be participant to travel to Scotland. Deer in English parks were for ornamental purposes, not to satisfy an instinct for the stealthy quest of one's quarry and ensuing slaughter which took many to the Highlands. Deer stalking was not as popular as game shooting and aroused more reservations about its merits. Lady Randolph Churchill wrote that although she saw no harm in a woman shooting,

> I cannot say I admire it as an accomplishment. The fact is, I love life so much that the unnecessary curtailing of any creature's existence is more than distasteful to me. Not long ago, while in Scotland, I saw a young and charming woman, who was surely not of a blood-thirsty nature, kill two stags in one morning. The first she shot through the heart. With the aid of a powerful pair of field-glasses, I watched her stalk the second. First she crawled on all-fours up a long burn; emerging hot and panting, not to say wet and dirty, she then continued her scramble up a steep hill, taking advantage of any cover afforded by the ground, or remaining in a petrified attitude if by chance a hind

happened to look up. The stag, meanwhile, quite oblivious of the danger lurking at hand, was apparently enjoying himself. Surrounded by his hinds, he trusted to their vigilance, and lay in the bracken in the brilliant sunshine. I could just see his fine antlered head, when suddenly, realising that all was not well, he bounded up, making a magnificent picture as he stood gazing round, his head thrown back in defiance. *Crash! Bang!* and this glorious animal became a maimed and tortured thing. Shot through both forelegs, he attempted to gallop down the hill, his poor broken limbs tumbling about him, while the affrighted hinds stood riveted to the spot, looking at their lord and master with horror, not unmixed with curiosity. I shall never forget the sight, or that of the dogs set on him, and the final scene, over which I draw a veil. If these things must be done, how can a woman bring herself to do them?

This is the end of a day's stalking in Glen Tilt on the Atholl estates *c.*1880.

By courtesy of the Duke of Atholl

The Braemar Gathering originated as the annual day of
revelry and walk of the Braemar Wright Friendly
Society, founded in 1817 by three carpenters. By dealing
in meal and careful husbandry, the society built up
sufficient resources to help the poor, sick, bereaved and
orphaned in the parish. Until 1896 these meetings were
often held at Braemar Castle where a dinner and ball
were held at the invitation of the Lairds of Invercauld.
The small arena before the castle was replaced by the
present ground of over 12 acres given to the Braemar
Royal Highland Society, as it became in 1866, by the 1st
Duke of Fife, whose family were patrons from the
earliest days. Athletic competitions began in 1832, and
the neighbouring nobility were quick to lend their
support in this revival of Highland traditions. In 1848,
Queen Victoria watched the games under the 'pretty
little castle' as she described it, and in 1859 the
gathering was held at Balmoral for the first time. This is
the scene at Braemar of the 1873 gathering.

By courtesy of the Duke of Atholl

The Leander Eight at Greenlands, a house on the river at Henley-on-Thames in Oxfordshire in the 1880s. The gentleman in the middle row and second from the left is the 2nd Viscount Hambleden, whose sister married the 5th Earl of Harrowby. Hambleden (born William Frederick Danvers Smith in 1868) was son of the W.H. Smith who had created what was then primarily a large chain of railway bookstalls. An equally able politician, W.H. Smith became 1st Lord of the Treasury and Leader of the House of Commons. In 1891 he relinquished his constituency of the Strand division of Westminster, handing over to William Frederick who held the seat for a further 19 years.

By courtesy of the Earl of Harrowby

The density of country houses and churches in East Anglia is exceptional and was a reflection of the area's prosperity, partly due to the influx of skilled workers from the Continent, many of whom were victims of religious persecution. It is the frequency with which the traveller in Norfolk or Suffolk meets the modest-sized house that is so remarkable. Bowthorpe Hall, near Norwich, was an adaptation of an older house, the projecting wing on the left being all that survives, while the main part of the hall was built *c*.1700. The photograph is thought to have been taken during the 1860s when croquet was the most popular outdoor sport. The game is believed to have originated in Languedoc as early as the thirteenth century. In the seventeenth century it became popular with the royal families of France before crossing the channel to England, where it was again popularised by the royal family. By the 1870s/80s, it was the usual game for the country house and garden party until displaced by lawn tennis.

Norwich Library

A group of spectators in the officers' enclosure at Blenheim Palace for the yeomanry sports held on 5 June 1911, including Winston Churchill under the umbrella; it was in that year that Churchill was appointed 1st Lord of the Admiralty with the instruction from Asquith to put the fleet into a state of readiness for war. Five thousand men of the Berkshire, Buckinghamshire and Oxfordshire yeomanries had been encamped in the grounds at Blenheim for the previous ten days. King Manuel of Portugal was staying with the Duke of Marlborough and had reviewed a parade by the brigades on the morning of the 5th. Thousands gathered in the grounds for the afternoon sports, and the *Oxford Journal Illustrated* remarked that 'it was a brilliant spectacle, the different uniforms contrasting gaily with the bright dresses of the ladies, and the officers' enclosure presented a very bright appearance.' Competitions included individual tent-pegging, horse racing and jumping, and a tug of war. Clementine Churchill had just given birth to Randolph, and Winston wrote to her: 'I have been out drilling all the morning and my poor face is already a sufferer from the sun. We have three regiments here, two just outside the ornamental garden, and the 3rd over by Bladon. I have 104 men in the squadron [Henley]. We are going to bathe in the lake this evening.' A ball in the palace for King Manuel concluded the day.

Radio Times Hulton Picture Library

Mrs Albu fencing with an unrecorded adversary at her
house-party on 17 September 1911 at Knebworth. This
was one of the periods when the house had been let, a
common practice when it was usual to have several
houses. The estate was then held by Victor 2nd Earl of
Lytton. The original late-fifteenth-century house has
been much altered over the centuries, notably by the
novelist Edward Bulwer-Lytton whose Gothic fantasies
have since had to be moderated to the exigencies of a
more austere age.

Radio Times Hulton Picture Library

Left: Sir Frederick Milner and the Countess of Pembroke at the house-party of Mr and Mrs Almeric Paget at Panshanger in July 1914. Sir Frederick Milner Bt, whose home was at Nun Appleton Hall, near Tadcaster in Yorkshire, was born in 1849 and served as a J.P. and Deputy Lieutenant for the West Riding. Beatrice Eleanor was sister to the 6th Marquess of Anglesey and married the future 15th Earl of Pembroke in 1904. She was grandmother of the present Earl. Lawn tennis became the fashionable game for country-house parties in the 1880s, displacing croquet in popularity. Until the invention of lawn tennis by an Englishman, Major Walter Wingfield, the game of tennis had been played only on walled and roofed courts. As building operations increased with industrialisation and urbanisation, many courts were demolished and the popularity of the game waned. It was in 1874 that Wingfield devised and patented 'a new and improved portable court for playing the ancient game of tennis'. The first championship was contested by 22 players and organised in 1877 by the England Croquet Club at its Wimbledon ground, adding 'Lawn Tennis' to its title. The Lawn Tennis Association was founded in 1886.

Radio Times Hulton Picture Library

It is ironic that photographs of servants actually doing something are extremely rare; it is even unusual to have the tools of their trade with them. This is a group of some of the Duchess of Kent's staff at Frogmore in Berkshire in 1861, the year that she died. It was at Frogmore that Queen Charlotte had found sanctuary from the pressures of life at Windsor with the attacks of insanity which beset George III. She established there her own farm, printing press and book bindery. The Duchess of Kent was the widow of the fourth son of George III and mother of Queen Victoria. At first buried alongside her husband at St George's Chapel, she was then moved to the elaborate mausoleum at Frogmore which her only child built for herself and Prince Albert at a cost of £200,000. Soon after their marriage, the household of the Duke and Duchess of Kent consisted of a Comptroller, 5 Grooms of the Bedchamber (3 of whom were Major Generals), 5 Equerries, 3 private secretaries (2 of whom were for charities), 1 librarian, 17 chaplains, 14 extra chaplains, 6 physicians, 3 physicians to the household, 1 physician extra, 7 surgeons, 5 surgeons to the household, 1 surgeon extra, 2 occulists, 1 aurist, 1 dentist, 2 apothecaries, 1 house steward and butler, 2 account clerks, 2 valets, 1 cook, 1 female housekeeper, 2 dressers for the Duchess, 1 head coachman, 1 head groom, 1 bookseller, 1 stationer. In comparison with those of his brothers, the Duke of Kent's household was modest. After the death of the Duke of Kent, the Duchess incurred the dislike of King William IV for the pomp and circumstance with which she surrounded her progresses round the Isle of Wight, exacting royal salutes from king's ships and batteries, albeit under the prompting of the unpleasant Sir John Conroy. 'The popping must stop', said the king. Frogmore was later the home of Queen Victoria's third daughter and mother of Princess Marie Louise before becoming a family museum.

Reproduced by gracious permission of Her Majesty The Queen

The household and outdoor staff at High Ashurst,
Surrey, in the 1890s. High Ashurst was the home of the
Hon. Henry Dudley-Ryder, only brother of the Earl of
Harrowby, and a partner in Coutts Bank. Before 1914
domestic employment accounted for a significant
percentage of the population and was an esteemed
occupation, not least for the conditions that compared
favourably with most others. Employment was not
subject to the vagaries of the trade cycle, living
conditions were generally good, servants could expect
leftovers of food and clothing, and it was customary for
guests to tip servants. The influx of radical ideas
fomented by the French Revolution had affected urban
centres rather than rural communities, and the natural
attitude of unquestioning deference towards the
aristocracy and landowners was hardly eroded during
the nineteenth century. Rural communities still looked to
the local landowner as their focal point, as the fountain
head of charity, and the occasion for festivities
commemorating a birth or coming-of-age in the noble
family. Although the long traditions of public service
and local benefaction were slowly waning with the
growth of municipalisation and county councils, they
were sufficiently strong to negate any criticisms of the
aristocracy as an obsolete group enjoying undeserved
privileges.

By courtesy of the Earl of Harrowby

The servants at Barton Court, situated between
Lymington and Christchurch in Hampshire. It was at a
house of this size that the younger servants—footmen,
pages and maids—would begin, rise by promotion and
move to a larger house. The number of servants was
important, not only to ensure the smooth and efficient
running of the house, but also to impress visitors and
enhance the standing of the family in the
neighbourhood. The idea was a relic of the feudal system
in which the power and influence of a knight or baron
was determined by the number of soldiers who owed
him their allegiance, and the horses that he could place
in the field. Nonetheless the nineteenth century saw a
very small contraction in the number of servants
employed, particularly from the 1880s. This was in
contrast to the proliferation of rooms in Victorian houses,
which contained separate rooms for ever more specialist
functions and facilitated segregation of the sexes, at least
when not at work. At Lanhydrock in Cornwall, for
example, a separate staircase was provided for the use of
female servants when the house was rebuilt in the 1880s.
Liveries were less common too. Numbers in the larger
houses, however, remained prodigious; on the Duke of
Rutland's birthday 145 servants sat down to dinner and
speeches; at Chatsworth the usual number in the
steward's room and servant's hall was 150; and 600
persons were on the direct payroll of the Duke of
Bedford.

By courtesy of the Earl of Harrowby

Right: Servants at Hinchingbrooke, home of the Earl of Sandwich, in 1906. It is difficult today to visualise the influence exercised by a sizable house over the locality. A visit to a country house may remind one that they may have embraced farms, gardens, dairies, brewhouses, granaries, stables, laundries, cellars, lime kilns, occasionally a brick kiln and more commonly a tilery to produce earthenware drain pipes for the estate; to maintain which the landowners would often employ full-time carpenters, ironmongers, painters, masons, smiths and glaziers, besides the people needed to run the many and varied aspects of the estate. But what such a visit does not recall is the close relationship between a landowner and the community; on the Duke of Rutland's birthday, for example, it was customary for the Duke to provide beef and ale in the villages around Belvoir to accompany dancing and music and the ringing of church bells throughout the Vale.

Huntingdon County Record Office

Below: The staff at Columbine Hall, Stowupland in Suffolk, *c*.1860, which was part of the Ashburnham estate. Even quite modest households, such as Columbine, would consume great quantities of food, and in times when retailing was a good deal less sophisticated than today it was usual for a house to have substantial stores in hand.

Suffolk Photographic Survey

Below right: Mr Edward Lay with a donkey-hauled lawnmower at Bramford Hall, Suffolk. Even the smaller country houses would have several full-time gardeners, although doubtless little distinction was made between work that needed doing on the estate and within the formal garden around the house. The head gardener of the larger houses occupied an esteemed position in the hierarchical structure of the Victorian household. Paxton's relationship with the Duke of Devonshire was exceptional, but it indicates the respect accorded to the horticulturist in an age devoted to elaborate gardens. The responsibility of the position is also indicated by the number of gardeners employed at larger houses – Welbeck had 53.

Suffolk Record Office

Scything the grass at Newark Castle near Maybole, Ayrshire, photographed soon after its restoration by the Marquess of Ailsa in the 1850s. Once a moated castle which withstood attacks during the long private war between the houses of Cassillis and Bargany following the slaughter of Sir Thomas Kennedy in 1602, Newark was totally remodelled in the 1850s, additions being made to the west and north sides which entailed the removal of many old features of the building. The marquessate was created in 1831, when the 12th Earl of Cassillis, whose principal residence was Culzean Castle, was made 1st Marquess.

   Meaning 'new work', it is not surprising that there were a number of Newark Castles—the Maxwell House at Port Glasgow, the Duke of Buccleuch's tower near Bowhill, besides Lord Newark's pile near St Monans in Fife.

                                    Lt Commander John Hamilton

Lord St Levan's boatmen, attired in their eighteenth-century uniform of red skirted coats, cream petticoats and leather helmets. They rowed his Lordship across the water from his home at St Michael's Mount to Marazion when the causeway was under water. Edward the Confessor established a religious foundation on the mount to mark the appearance of St Michael one night in 495 and the building became a fortress in the fifteenth century. After the Civil War it came to the St Aubyn family, who gave the castle to the National Trust in 1954. Queen Victoria and Prince Albert visited the Mount in 1846, but it was during a dispute between the 15 illegitimate children of the late 5th Sir John St Aubyn over his will, so there was nobody to receive them. Nonetheless, Prince Albert tried the church organ which he pronounced 'very fine'. St Michael's Mount is one of a small number of country houses which receives supplies by railway, in this case underground from the bottom of the mount. Pack horses formerly performed the task.

                        Museum of English Rural Life, University of Reading

Until the eighteenth century, journeys to country houses from London were uncomfortable and slow. When Elizabeth I travelled to Ingatestone Hall to stay with one of her counsellors, Sir William Petrie, she did so in an unsprung carriage which often became bogged down in mud. The invention of springing and improvement of roads by turnpike trusts made country-house visiting and expeditions from London a much more acceptable proposition. The changing attitude to travel was reflected in the increasing size of parties and balls at country houses, in turn demanding larger rooms. This phaeton is seen outside Cawdor Castle, the dramatic home of the earls of Cawdor, one of the few buildings mentioned in Shakespeare which is still inhabited. Foot warmers, long flat tins with a covering of carpet, were filled with boiling water and placed on the floor of carriages for winter journeys. A stone-pick for the horses' hooves was an equally necessary accoutrement. Carriages were often equipped with a 'shoe', a heavy iron skid which was hung on a chain beneath the floor. It was applied to one of the wheels when descending steep hills and its

adjustment was a tricky affair. Still less agreeable was its removal at the foot of the hill, by which time it had grown dangerously hot and awkward to handle. Replacing the shoe on its hook was an unenviable task, with an arm through the spokes of a well-muddied wheel while the horses fidgeted and threatened to crush an unskilled hand.

By courtesy of the Earl of Cawdor

A landau at Stoke Edith Park, Herefordshire, in October 1891. Seated in the carriage are the Duke and Duchess of Teck, Princess May of Teck and P. Foley; behind it, from left to right, are Miss W. Herbert, Sir Andrew Scobell, Lady Emily Foley, and Mr Montgomery. Lady Emily Foley, a daughter of the 3rd Duke of Montrose, had married Edward Foley, M.P. for the county of Hereford, in 1832. He died without issue in 1846, leaving Lady Emily a long widowhood. The house had been largely built by 1698 for Paul Foley, although Sir James Thornhill was still at work decorating the Great Hall with colossal murals in 1705, and the grounds were later laid out by Repton. In the 1850s an intricate geometric parterre was created by Nesfield. But this splendour was laid waste by a fire which virtually destroyed the house in 1927. No attempt was made to rebuild it and the gardens were left to nature to refashion.

Reproduced by gracious permission of Her Majesty the Queen

Overleaf: A four-in-hand meeting at Keith Hall when the Gordon Highlanders were there on 26 September 1899. Keith Hall is the home of the earls of Kintore. Built by Sir John Keith, 1st Earl, in the late seventeenth century, the house was extensively altered by the 9th Countess in the late nineteenth century when she constructed an extraordinary stone-vaulted baronial dining room. The two bay windows were added at the same time.

By courtesy of the Earl of Kintore

A pony and trap held by David Bruce (1888–1964), fourth son of the 9th Earl of Elgin, in the grounds of his home at Broomhall near Dunfermline c.1895. He was to serve as a colonel in the Seaforth Highlanders during World War I and became a Deputy Lieutenant of Sutherland. In the cart are three of the daughters of the 9th Earl, Christain, Marjorie, and Rachel. The 9th Earl was married to the second daughter of the 9th Countess of Southesk who is pictured in the photograph on **page 29**.

By courtesy of the Earl of Elgin

A group of Talbots are seen here in front of Ingestre Hall in September 1903. Four years later Edward VII visited the hall, on which occasion eight Talbots were in use.

The 20th Earl of Shrewsbury and Talbot and Premier Earl of England was born in 1860, succeeding to the title in 1877. No aristocrat did more for road transport in its infancy: for some years he operated the Greyhound coach from Buxton to Alton Towers, one of his residences; he was involved in the establishment of the Clement-Talbot Company in 1903, later British Talbot, of which he was chairman; and he established the first taxi cab service in Paris and London to use noiseless tyres. He was an early victim of police speed traps, of which there were so many on the Brighton road that the A.A. was founded in 1905 to warn drivers of their presence. The speed limit was then 20 m.p.h., and in 1908 the *Daily Telegraph* reported that 'at Dumbarton the Earl of Shrewsbury and Talbot was convicted of excessive driving near Garelockhead, and was fined 3 guineas. The Earl covered a measured $\frac{1}{2}$ mile in 58 seconds, giving a speed of 31 m.p.h.' His principal residence was Ingestre Hall, a magnificent Jacobean house of which the rooms behind the façade had been reinstated after fire had gutted them in October 1882.

National Motor Museum, Beaulieu

Roland Kitson and his father, Lord Airedale, outside the family home at Gledhow Hall near Leeds. The car is a 1903/4 60 h.p. Mercedes which was the sports-touring car *par excellence* of the veteran era with a 4084 c.c. engine. Roland Kitson represented the third generation in the family's rise to prosperity: his grandfather, James Kitson (1807–85), had been an inn keeper, but through his inventiveness, diligence and some good fortune, he established the Airedale Foundry, became Mayor of Leeds and a director of the North Eastern Railway and the Yorkshire Banking Co.; his father, also depicted in the photograph on **page 30**, was raised to the peerage in 1907. Roland (1882–1958) was the first to have the customary education of a young gentleman – public school and Oxbridge. He served in World War I, afterwards becoming a director of the Ford Motor Co. and the Bank of England. His half-brother became 2nd Baron, and Roland Kitson succeeded to the title in 1944. Gledhow Hall was put up in the early nineteenth century and has been attributed to John Carr, better known for the design of Harewood House.

Leeds City Library

Right: On 29 October 1900 Victoria Mary, Duchess of York, made her 'first drive in a motor! to visit Raglan' in the company of the Hon. Charles Stewart Rolls (1877–1910), Lady Llangattock, his mother, on the left, and Lady Eva Dugdale. Lady Eva Dugdale was the daughter of the 4th Earl of Warwick and had married Col Frank Dugdale of the well-known Warwickshire family whose seat was at Wroxall Abbey near the county town. Lady Dugdale was Extra Woman of the Bedchamber to Queen Mary. The son of the 1st Baron Llangattock, Charles Rolls went to Eton and Cambridge and, in the same year as this drive, he was awarded a gold medal for his performance in the 1,000 miles trial between London and Edinburgh and back. Charles Rolls was fascinated by anything of a mechanical nature, beginning his experiments with a disused bath chair at The Hendre and graduating to the steam roller on his father's estate. His first acquaintance with cars was in France before the Act of 1896 legalised their use on British roads. The portentous meeting between the engineering perfectionist Henry Royce and Charles Rolls took place in 1904 at Royce's works in Manchester. An agreement was made whereby Rolls would sell all the cars produced by Royce, and by the end of the year, the first Rolls-Royce was exhibited at the Paris exhibition. Another interest was flying, and in July 1910 he crashed in the Wright triplane which he had flown to Calais and back. As *The Times* expressed it, Rolls was the first Englishman 'who has sacrificed his life in the cause of modern aviation'.

Reproduced by gracious permission of
Her Majesty the Queen

The former stable block and fleet of motor cars at Pell
Wall House near Market Drayton in 1911. The house was
the seat of the Griffin family, who also owned nearby
Brand Hall. The car in the garage is a Renault, or a
Cheswold, while in the yard is a Rolls Royce Silver
Ghost tourer on the left and a Mercedes limousine on the
right. Membership of the A.A. is proclaimed on the last
two. The advent of the motor car came at a most
propitious moment for landed society. The 20 to 30 years
before World War I were a time of falling agricultural
revenues, slowly increasing taxation and rising labour
costs. So the opportunity to reduce the often sizable
stable staff must have been a blessing to those who
regarded horses as a means of transport rather than a
source of pleasure.

Couzins/Powney Collection and National Motor Museum

The 8th and last Earl of Sandwich (1839–1916) seated in his Daimler in 1907. A lieutenant-colonel in the Grenadier Guards, he accompanied the Prince of Wales on a tour of Canada and the USA in 1860. He entered the diplomatic service and was attached to the embassies in Berlin and Königsberg before returning home to become M.P. for Huntingdon and to take on the traditional roles, for eminent landowners, of lord-lieutenant and high steward of the county. He went abroad again in 1874 as attaché to Lord Sydney's special embassy to St Petersburg for the marriage of Queen Victoria's second son, the Duke of Edinburgh, to the Grand Duchess Marie Alexandrovna, daughter of Alexander II. His home at Hinchingbrooke, near Huntingdon, was originally an eleventh-century Augustinian nunnery. It had only its prioress and three nuns when it was suppressed by Henry VIII and given to Sir Richard Williams, alias Cromwell. The house grew during the sixteenth and seventeenth centuries and was sold by Sir Oliver Cromwell in 1627 to Sir Sidney Montagu whose son became Viscount Hinchingbrooke and Earl of Sandwich. The house was extensively remodelled after a fire in the 1830s by Edward Blore, about whom Pevsner is scathing: 'He was a dull man; Hinchingbrooke confirms it.'

Huntingdon County Records Office

The way so many country houses have gone: Gordon Castle in Morayshire, home of the dukes of Gordon, was reduced in 1955. Standing in a spacious park of 1,300 acres, formerly a marsh called the Bog of Gight, the castle passed to the Duke of Richmond in 1836, the title of Duke of Gordon being revived in his favour in 1876. It was the largest mansion in the area, measuring over 600 feet in length, and incorporated a 90-foot-high square tower of fifteenth-century origin.

Scottish Record Office and Royal Commission on the Ancient & Historical Monuments of Scotland